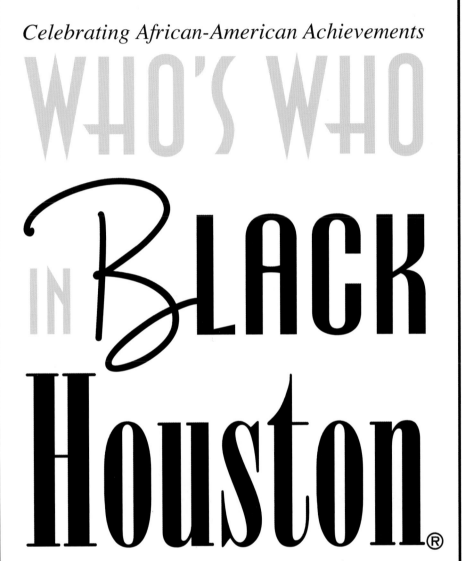

Celebrating African-American Achievements

WHO'S WHO
in BLACK
Houston®
THE FIFTH EDITION

Celebrating African-American Achievements

WHO'S WHO

In BLACK

Houston®

THE FOURTH EDITION

A Real Times Media Company

Who's Who In Black Houston®
is a registered trademark of
Real Times Media

Purchase additional copies online @
www.whoswhopublishing.com

Corporate Headquarters
Who's Who Publishing Co.
3700 Corporate Drive, Suite 110
Columbus, Ohio 43231

All Credit Cards Accepted
*Inquiries for bulk purchases for youth
groups, schools, churches, civic or
professional organizations, please call
our office for volume discounts.*

Corporate Headquarters
(614) 481-7300

Photo Credits
Ken Jones

Cover Design by: Chris Friason

ISBN # 978-1-935601-26-5 Hardback
$50.00 each-U.S. Hardback
Commemorative Edition

ISBN # 978-1-935601-25-8 Paperback
$34.95 each-U.S. Paperback

TABLE OF
CONTENTS

7
Frank Stewart

11
Judson Robinson III

42
The Johnson Family

58
Laurence Humphries

62

Jackie Lathan Phillips

Welcome 2011 Who's Who in Black Houston

Four 3,000-square-foot balconies overlook Discovery Green, offering a stunning view from above.

Indoor-outdoor terraces offer a unique setting for receptions with a panoramic view of downtown as the backdrop.

One of the largest ballrooms in Houston, the 31,590-square-foot Grand Ballroom seats 2,100 comfortably and may be divided into three equal sections.

Introduction by

Frank Stewart
President, American Association of Blacks in Energy

It was nearly four decades ago that OPEC, the Organization of the Petroleum Exporting Countries, initiated its oil embargo, taught the western world a great lesson in economics and ushered in a heightened awareness of and appreciation for the role of energy in all our lives. At that time petroleum was the fuel that powered virtually all of our transportation, was the source of much of our electricity, and was a significant energy resource for our industry. As the United States scrambled to find means to keep its economy from crumbling, it became abundantly clear that the embargo was not only an economic threat, but an international policy and a national security threat as well. While the United States celebrated its 200th birthday, the president and his team were busy developing the first National Energy Plan.

The president's energy policy team included no person of color, and the plan that was developed only minimally acknowledged the particular importance that energy plays in the minority communities across the nation. Indeed people of color in the leadership of the energy industries were very, very few. Moreover, neither the energy industry nor the government appreciated that communities of color paid a dramatically higher percentage of their disposable income for energy, that communities of color are significantly more vulnerable to the negative impact related to a rise in the price of energy, and that those communities bear a disproportionately higher negative economic and health impact from energy decisions.

It was against this 1977 backdrop that the American Association of Blacks in Energy was founded. It was against this backdrop that those whom you will meet in this publication began to make their presence felt.

Today Houston, Texas, is still the energy capitol of the nation. Houston is the headquarters of 26 of the largest corporations in the world and of those, 13 are energy companies. Of the Fortune 100 fastest growing companies in the nation, eight are headquartered in Houston and of the eight companies, six are energy companies. Whether it is oil, or gas, or nuclear, or wind, Houston is home to some of the leading energy companies in the world.

The growth of black Americans in Houston is the growth of the black Americans in the energy industry, and over the last quarter of a century, that growth has been remarkable. Although high-tech companies are an important force in Houston, energy companies dominate in virtually every measure.

The advancement of blacks in corporate America is one of the most important business stories of the last 25 years. Nowhere is that story told more clearly than in Houston, Texas. But the story is not over. At the beginning of this second decade of the 21st century we are on the cusp of a national transformation of our energy systems. As the nation moves to a more carbon efficient energy system, black Houston is poised to play a very important role. As we move to the use of more sophisticated technologies to deliver the products needed to fuel our transportation and our industry, black Houston is poised to play a leading role. As we move to rebuild both the electric grid and the network of gas pipelines, black Houston could well be a leader in that area too.

In the following pages you will meet much of the economic, cultural, social and intellectual leadership in Houston. These men and women continue to be a source of pride, inspiration and aspiration for us all. Their achievements of the past and their vision for the future will help to define the role that black Americans play not only in Houston, but across these United States.

Frank Stewart

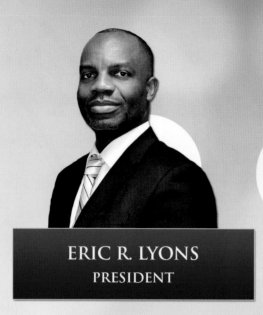

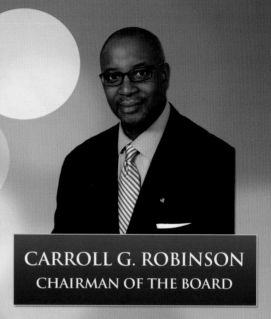

ERIC R. LYONS
PRESIDENT

CARROLL G. ROBINSON
CHAIRMAN OF THE BOARD

HOUSTON CITIZENS CHAMBER OF COMMERCE
ACCESS - ADVOCACY - AWARENESS

THE HOUSTON CITIZENS CHAMBER SALUTES
ALL OF THE

WHO'S WHO IN BLACK HOUSTON
HONOREES

WE INVITE EVERYONE TO ENGAGE IN THE PROGRAMS
AND EVENTS OF OUR ORGANIZATION INCLUDING THE

2011 AFRICAN AMERICAN BUSINESS ACHIEVEMENT PINNACLE AWARDS

THAT WILL BE HELD ON FRIDAY, OCTOBER 14, 2011.
VISIT WWW.HCCCPINNACLEAWARDS.ORG
FOR ADDITIONAL DETAILS.

HOUSTON
CITIZENS CHAMBER
FOUNDATION

WWW.HCCOC.ORG

We recognize what you've accomplished … and who you inspire.

∙∙

Congratulations to this year's Who's Who in Black Houston honorees. Reliant Energy is proud to support **Who's Who** and to help shine a light on the deserving individuals being recognized.

1-866-RELIANT / *reliant.com*

MEET OUR TEAM

WHO'S Who

A Real Times Media Company

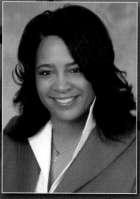

Vernita Harris
Houston Associate Publisher

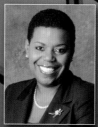

Cassandra F. Bozeman
Chief Operating Officer

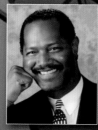

Ernie Sullivan
Executive Vice President

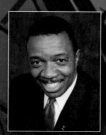

Carter Womack
Vice President of Market Development

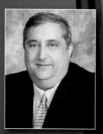

Brian Auler
Business Manager

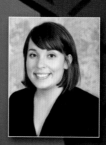

Meagan Culley
Communications Manager

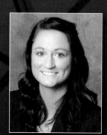

Kimberly Byers
Graphic Designer

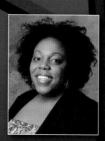

Donna Marbury
Copy Editor

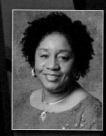

Karen Perkins
Copy Editor

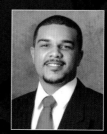

Chris Friason
Graphic Designer

CORPORATE OFFICE

3700 Corporate Drive, Suite 110 • Columbus, Ohio 43231 • (614) 481-7300

www.whoswhopublishing.com

Foreword by

JUDSON W. ROBINSON III

Chief Executive Officer & President
Houston Area Urban League

It is a special honor to join the tradition of **Who's Who In Black Houston**® in its fifth edition by following the previous writers – Gerald B. Smith, Anthony Hall Jr., Dr. Mae C. Jemison and last year's author, Dr. John M. Rudley, as they have continued as role models for the Houston community.

I would first like to congratulate the honorees who have been selected for inclusion. Your successes are great and your perseverance unwavering. I would also like to thank Who's Who Publishing Company for producing positive and community-oriented publications that foster our youth and emphasize the necessity of diversity.

Houston has a history of being one of the most powerful cities in the nation. Iconic monuments such as the Spindletop, which made us the energy capital of the world; the Port of Houston Authority, one of the busiest in the world and our bayou systems make us prime for trade and have assisted our growth in becoming the fourth largest city in the country.

We are also a city where men and women of various colors and beliefs have equal opportunity and have achieved high positions in elected office, corporations, medical institutions, prominent boards, universities, and science and space.

Although this city has made strides in greatness and change, we must desire to be the best. We must not settle for two societies – the haves and have-nots. Nonprofit organizations like the Houston Area Urban League specialize in helping people become self-sufficient and contribute to the economic engine of our society by maximizing their human potential. Our energy-centered community must continue to participate aggressively in building a diverse future in order to maintain success. This is possible by continuing to support STEM technology and assisting low-performing schools where ZIP codes determine teacher and school quality. As a leader in energy production, the city of Houston must also continue to be a leader in pushing diversity through doors that were once unavailable to African Americans.

Our vision of becoming partners of diversity will be achieved by promoting the capabilities and commitment of citizens like you. We can show the world what is possible right here, in the city of Houston.

We have much to be proud of. Let us continue to find ways to express this pride throughout our communities.

I once again salute all individuals listed in this fifth edition of **Who's Who In Black Houston**® and encourage this group of leaders to seize the privilege of service and aggressively lead our community into its future.

Sincerely,

Judson W. Robinson III

CORPORATE SPONSORS

OFFICIAL AIRLINE

DIAMOND SPONSOR

EMERALD SPONSORS

UNVEILING SPONSORS

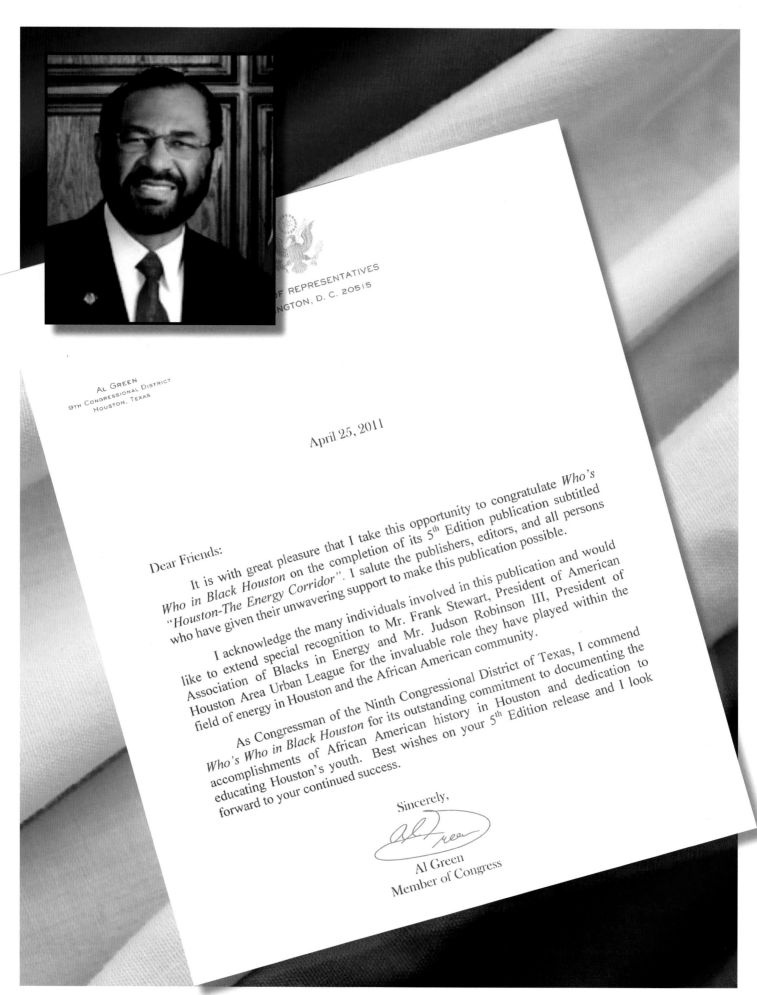

OF REPRESENTATIVES
NGTON, D. C. 20515

AL GREEN
9TH CONGRESSIONAL DISTRICT
HOUSTON, TEXAS

April 25, 2011

Dear Friends:

It is with great pleasure that I take this opportunity to congratulate *Who's in Black Houston* on the completion of its 5th Edition publication subtitled *"Houston-The Energy Corridor"*. I salute the publishers, editors, and all persons who have given their unwavering support to make this publication possible.

I acknowledge the many individuals involved in this publication and would like to extend special recognition to Mr. Frank Stewart, President of American Association of Blacks in Energy and Mr. Judson Robinson III, President of Houston Area Urban League for the invaluable role they have played within the field of energy in Houston and the African American community.

As Congressman of the Ninth Congressional District of Texas, I commend *Who's Who in Black Houston* for its outstanding commitment to documenting the accomplishments of African American history in Houston and dedication to educating Houston's youth. Best wishes on your 5th Edition release and I look forward to your continued success.

Sincerely,

Al Green
Member of Congress

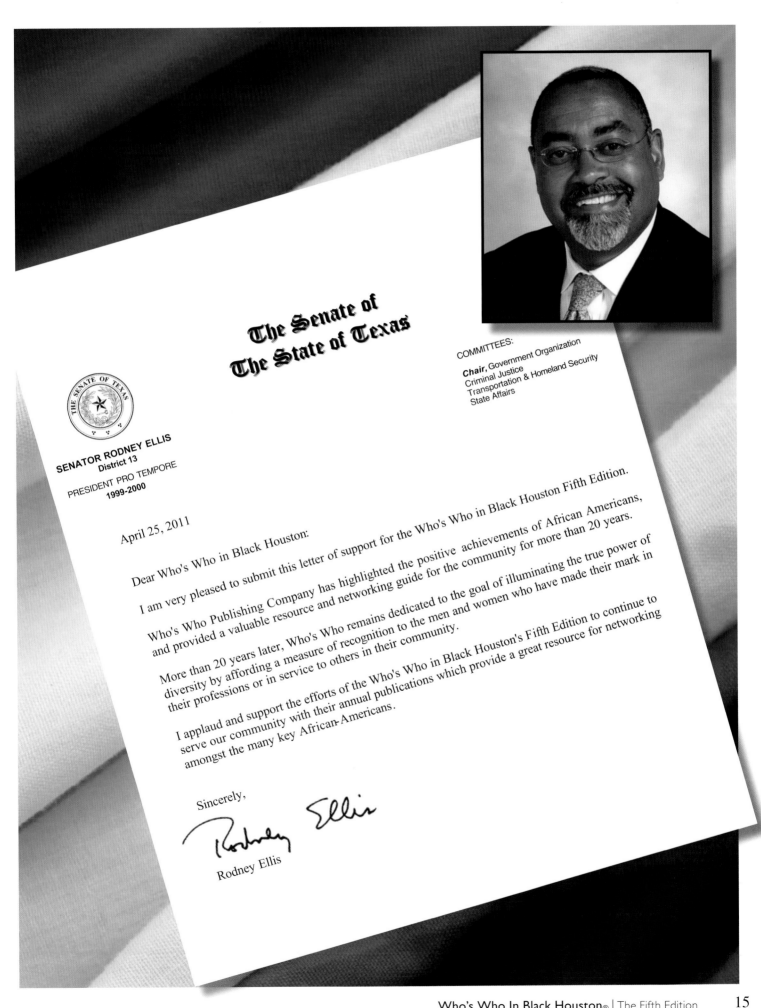

The Senate of
The State of Texas

COMMITTEES:

Chair, Government Organization
Criminal Justice
Transportation & Homeland Security
State Affairs

SENATOR RODNEY ELLIS
District 13
PRESIDENT PRO TEMPORE
1999-2000

April 25, 2011

Dear Who's Who in Black Houston:

I am very pleased to submit this letter of support for the Who's Who in Black Houston Fifth Edition.

Who's Who Publishing Company has highlighted the positive achievements of African Americans, and provided a valuable resource and networking guide for the community for more than 20 years.

More than 20 years later, Who's Who remains dedicated to the goal of illuminating the true power of diversity by affording a measure of recognition to the men and women who have made their mark in their professions or in service to others in their community.

I applaud and support the efforts of the Who's Who in Black Houston's Fifth Edition to continue to serve our community with their annual publications which provide a great resource for networking amongst the many key African-Americans.

Sincerely,

Rodney Ellis

Rodney Ellis

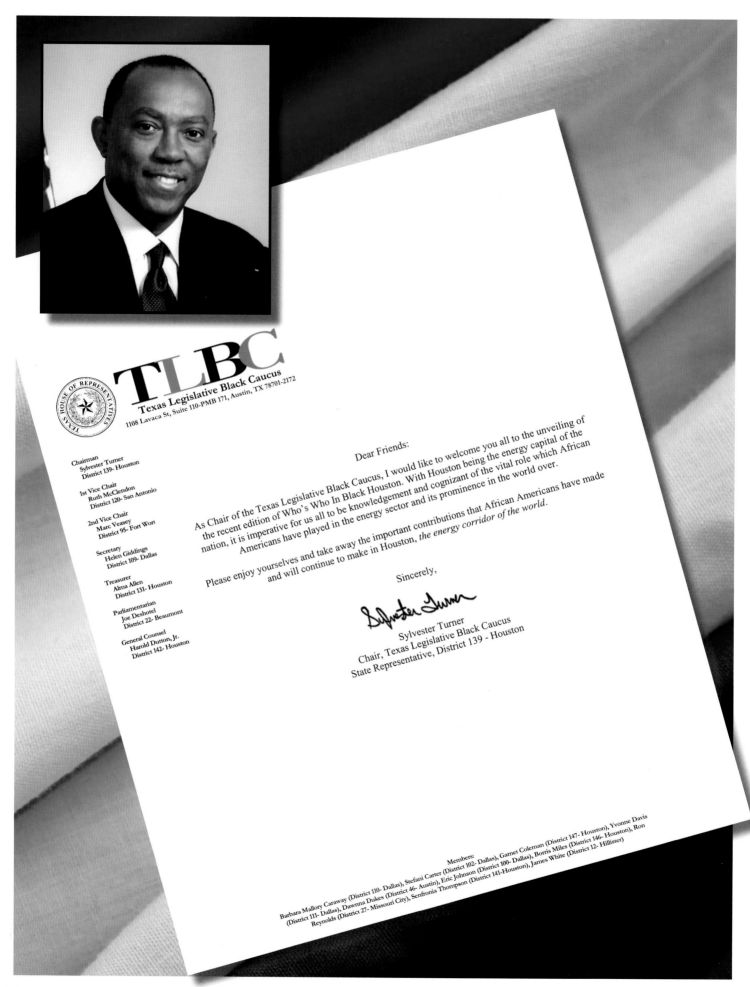

TLBC
Texas Legislative Black Caucus

TEXAS HOUSE OF REPRESENTATIVES

1108 Lavaca St, Suite 110-PMB 171, Austin, TX 78701-2172

Chairman
Sylvester Turner
District 139- Houston

1st Vice Chair
Ruth McClendon
District 120- San Antonio

2nd Vice Chair
Marc Veasey
District 95- Fort Wort

Secretary
Helen Giddings
District 109- Dallas

Treasurer
Alma Allen
District 131- Houston

Parliamentarian
Joe Deshotel
District 22- Beaumont

General Counsel
Harold Dutton, Jr.
District 142- Houston

Dear Friends:

As Chair of the Texas Legislative Black Caucus, I would like to welcome you all to the unveiling of the recent edition of Who's Who In Black Houston. With Houston being the energy capital of the nation, it is imperative for us all to be knowledgement and cognizant of the vital role which African Americans have played in the energy sector and its prominence in the world over.

Please enjoy yourselves and take away the important contributions that African Americans have made and will continue to make in Houston, *the energy corridor of the world*.

Sincerely,

Sylvester Turner
Chair, Texas Legislative Black Caucus
State Representative, District 139 - Houston

Members:
Barbara Mallory Caraway (District 110- Dallas), Garnet Coleman (District 147- Houston), Yvonne Davis (District 111- Dallas), Stefani Carter (District 102- Dallas), Borris Miles (District 146- Houston), Ron Reynolds (District 27- Missouri City), Senfronia Thompson (District 141-Houston), James White (District 12- Hillister)

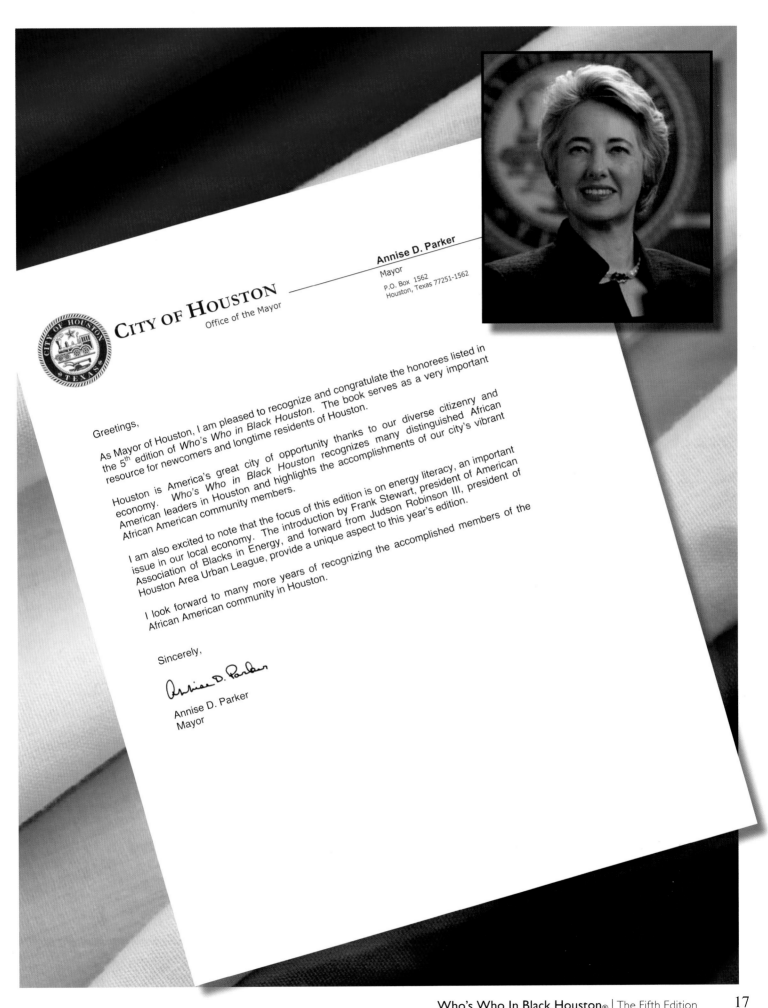

Annise D. Parker
Mayor

P.O. Box 1562
Houston, Texas 77251-1562

CITY OF HOUSTON
Office of the Mayor

Greetings,

As Mayor of Houston, I am pleased to recognize and congratulate the honorees listed in the 5th edition of *Who's Who in Black Houston*. The book serves as a very important resource for newcomers and longtime residents of Houston.

Houston is America's great city of opportunity thanks to our diverse citizenry and economy. *Who's Who in Black Houston* recognizes many distinguished African American leaders in Houston and highlights the accomplishments of our city's vibrant African American community members.

I am also excited to note that the focus of this edition is on energy literacy, an important issue in our local economy. The introduction by Frank Stewart, president of American Association of Blacks in Energy, and forward from Judson Robinson III, president of Houston Area Urban League, provide a unique aspect to this year's edition.

I look forward to many more years of recognizing the accomplished members of the African American community in Houston.

Sincerely,

Annise D. Parker
Mayor

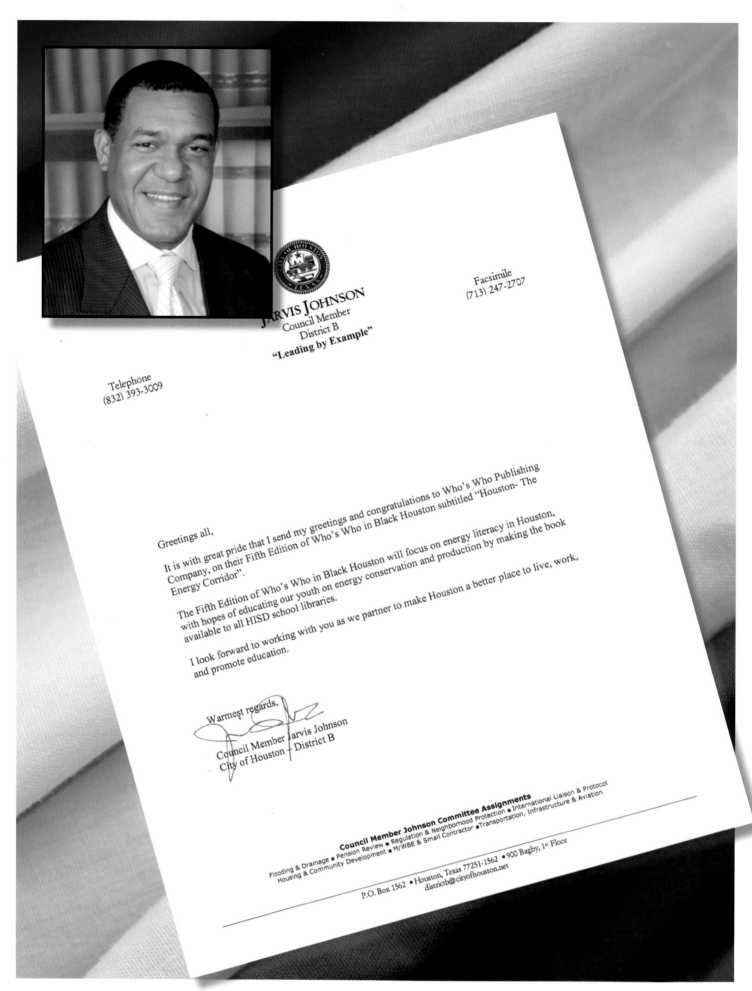

Facsimile
(713) 247-2707

JARVIS JOHNSON
Council Member
District B
"Leading by Example"

Telephone
(832) 393-3009

Greetings all,

It is with great pride that I send my greetings and congratulations to Who's Who Publishing Company, on their Fifth Edition of Who's Who in Black Houston subtitled "Houston- The Energy Corridor".

The Fifth Edition of Who's Who in Black Houston will focus on energy literacy in Houston, with hopes of educating our youth on energy conservation and production by making the book available to all HISD school libraries.

I look forward to working with you as we partner to make Houston a better place to live, work, and promote education.

Warmest regards,

Council Member Jarvis Johnson
City of Houston – District B

Council Member Johnson Committee Assignments
Flooding & Drainage ▪ Pension Review ▪ Regulation & Neighborhood Protection ▪ International Liaison & Protocol
Housing & Community Development ▪ M/WBE & Small Contractor ▪ Transportation, Infrastructure & Aviation

P.O. Box 1562 ▪ Houston, Texas 77251-1562 ▪ 900 Bagby, 1st Floor
districtb@cityofhouston.net

Houston City Council Member
District D

April 2011

Chair, Neighborhood Protection and Quality of Life
Budget and Fiscal Affairs
Flooding and Drainage
M/WBE and Small Contractor Development
Transportation, Infrastructure & Aviation

Vice-Chair Technology Initiatives and Human Services
Development and Regulatory Affairs
Housing & Community Development
Public Safety and Homeland Security

Dear Fellow Houstonians

It is an honor to be with you again. I write this letter yearly. It is more than a simple ritual, but more fittingly a celebration of a growing network becoming more cohesive and impactful year after year. I welcome the 5th edition Of *Who's Who in Black Houston*. This publication serves to not only showcase examples of excellence, but stories of perseverance. Confidently, it also speaks to the imperativeness of a close knit community willing to challenge our dependence on others.

As disparities widen in our access to capital, quality health care, sound infrastructure, and investments in education, it is a critical that we develop channels through which our own endeavors stabilize our own communities. This book speaks to that movement. Profiles of men and women in this edition successfully denote characteristics of intellect and consciousness cascading across varying professional fields.

Thank you for your continued efforts in highlighting the achievements of noteworthy professionals in Houston. We will continue to need these resources. We will continue to utilize publications like these to strengthen relationships and build upon a strong foundation.

We thank you. We need you. We wish you continued success.

Sincerely,

Wanda Adams
Wanda Adams
Houston City Council, District D
CITY HALL ANNEX 900 BAGBY, 1ST FLOOR
PHONE 832.393.3001

P.O. BOX 1562 HOUSTON TX 77251-1562
FAX 832.393.3201

DISTRICTD@HOUSTONTX.GOV
WWW.HOUSTONTX.GOV

CITY OF HOUSTON

OFFICE OF COUNCIL MEMBER JOLANDA "JO" JONES
AT-LARGE POSITION 5

April 2011

Greetings!

It is my pleasure to add my congratulations on the unveiling of Who's Who in Black Houston, 5th Edition. The book, subtitled "Houston-The Energy Corridor," will no doubt be a treasure for years to come.

I am so proud of the contributions the Who's Who organization has made in highlighting the accomplishments of African-Americans, particularly in my favorite city and hometown, Houston. I am also delighted that Reliant Energy has pledged to make a copy of the new Who's Who edition available to every HISD library. It is so important that young people of all ethnic and cultural backgrounds are exposed to positive role models as early as possible.

Again, congratulations!

The People Are The City,

Jolanda "Jo" Jones

Jolanda "Jo" Jones
Houston City Council
At-Large Position 5

COUNCIL COMMITTEES: HOUSING & COMMUNITY DEVELOPMENT – CHAIR ■ INTERNATIONAL BUSINESS INITIATIVES – CHAIR
FLOODING & DRAINAGE ■ BUDGET & FISCAL AFFAIRS ■ M/WBE & SMALL CONTRACTOR DEVELOPMENT
PUBLIC SAFETY & HOMELAND SECURITY ■ TRANSPORTATION, INFRASTRUCTURE & AVIATION

900 BAGBY ◆ HOUSTON, TX 77002 ◆ 832-393-3006 ◆ FAX 832-393-3261 ◆ ATLARGE5@HOUSTONTX.GOV

1,000 BOOKS *for* 1,000 KIDS
OUR MISSION

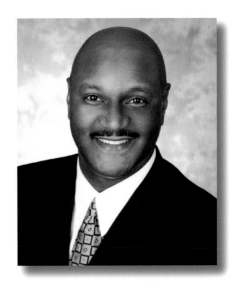

Greetings Fellow Houstonians:

I am very honored to have had the opportunity to serve as the first book ambassador for ***Who's Who In Black Houston®*** and lead the campaign to get this historic fifth edition in the hands of our girls and boys.

The Who's Who 1,000 Books for 1,000 Kids campaign brings awareness to children throughout Houston's metropolitan area by putting ***Who's Who In Black Houston®*** in the hands of elementary, middle and high school students. I believe that our boys and girls must have the opportunity to read about as well as see images of the outstanding African-American men and women featured in this fifth edition.

Giving back to the community is a passion of mine and to partner with ***Who's Who In Black Houston®*** for this 1,000 Books for 1,000 Kids campaign brings me full circle. I truly believe that strong positive role models will enhance our future generation's potential to be successful. Our goal is to always have the individuals in this edition make themselves available to visit schools, spend time with our young people and have real life discussions about themselves and what it takes to be successful in this global market place.

The challenge is before us and the opportunity awaits us. The emotional charge is hidden in the acronym of Who's Who. I have coined the new phrase to keep us motivate and on task: We Have Overcome, so, We Help Others (Who's Who).

I want to thank each individual and organization that supported our 1,000 Books for 1000 Kids program. As we continue to work in the Houston community to improve the quality of life, to get each citizen voting, and ensuring that children are getting the best education possible, we need good stewards like you be engaged and make things happen.

With Best Regards,

James Harris

James Harris
Book Ambassador

Leading Book Purchasers for Houston 5th Edition

Reliant Energy

The Varnett School

McConnell Jones Lanier & Murphy

Maurice and Stefanie Stone

Omar and Janice Reid

Terence and Diedra Fontaine

H.E.B.

Together we can uplift and inspire the next generation of leaders.

1,000 Books
for 1,000 Kids

The NCAA salutes you for hosting the 2011 and 2016 Men's Final Four. We're looking forward to a great time in Houston. Thanks for your hospitality!

NCAA.com

Amegy Bankers dedicated to the Success of Houston Business

JEVAUGHN STERLING
VP, CBP LENDING MANAGER

STACY BARNES
VP, BANKING CENTER MANAGER

LAYLA MISGINA
VP, BANKING CENTER MANAGER

KENYATTA GIBBS
VP, ENERGY LENDER

MICHAEL PEARSON
SVP, REAL ESTATE LENDER

BONNIE REED
VP, TREASURY SALES

LISA JOHNSON
VP, BANKING CENTER MANAGER

CARLOTTA FRANKLIN
VP, HR COMPENSATION

WINSTON LABBE
VP, COMMERCIAL LENDER

CRYSTAL FOARD
VP, PRODUCT MANAGER

DIANE MABEN
SVP, PRODUCT MANAGEMENT

DONNA KING
SVP, CREDIT RISK MANAGER

CHRIS CYPRIEN
VP, TREASURY PRODUCT MANAGEMENT

SHIRLEY PENN
VP, CRA LENDER

BRENDA COOPER
VP, HR BUSINESS PARTNER

Real Times Media was established out of a passion to provide the African-American community with information that enlightens, empowers and inspires. With a legacy stretching back over 100 years, we possess an unparalleled depth of knowledge and assets that are multi generational, relevant and trustworthy.

A true multi media company focused on becoming the leading source of news, entertainment and lifestyle information from the African-American perspective, Real Times Media provides comprehensive print content that helps our communities continue to thrive and grow while chronicling the events and individuals who are making history today.

We accomplish this through our various enterprises and interests which include:

- The most extensive African-American newspaper collective in the nation, including of the Chicago Defender, the Michigan Chronicle, The Michigan FrontPage, The New Pittsburgh Courier and the Tri-State Defender (Memphis)

- Who's Who Publishing Company, the creator of the largest portfolio of publications showcasing African-American professionals

- A full-service marketing and communications company providing strategy, production and management for ad campaigns, TV/Radio production, interactive, public relations, and event marketing and promotions

- RTM Digital Studios, which is focused on the creation, distribution and licensing of original content for book publishing and film/documentary projects using its extensive archive of historical photographs and other artifacts of the African-American experience throughout the past century

- A series of live events across the country that pay honor to unsung community, business, and religious leaders

Real Times Media is poised to realize a future as rich as the legacy which precedes it. With an unrivaled connection to traditionally hard-to-reach, affluent minority markets, we offer our clients a full range of targeted solutions for all of their multicultural marketing needs. Let us do the same for you. For more information, visit us online at www.realtimesmedia.com or call (313) 963-8100.

 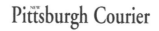 

A MESSAGE FROM THE
CEO
HIRAM E. JACKSON
REAL TIMES MEDIA

"There never were in the world two opinions alike, no more than two hairs or two grains; the most university quality is diversity."
– Michel de Montaigne

It is with great pride that I welcome you to the fifth anniversary edition of **Who's Who In Black Houston**®. For the past four years our publication has remained committed to delivering remarkable stories of high-achieving African Americans in the Houston metropolitan area. Throughout this journey, we have uncovered countless stories of extraordinary power, persistence, devotion and knowledge. Like all our editions, the individuals profiled in these pages represent some of the most dynamic talent in the country.

Our publications serve the community in many ways as we strive to highlight all aspects of success within the cities we touch. We do this not only to celebrate African-American achievement, but also to inspire future generations. Penning the foreword to this historic edition is Judson Robinson III, president and chief executive officer of the Houston Urban League, while Frank Stewart, president of the American Association of Blacks in Energy, writes this year's introduction. We would like to thank them for working tirelessly to promote the benefits and advantages Houston offers its residents.

As I close, I reflect upon the many opportunities that brought me to where I am today. All of these moments continue to inspire me as I persist in the Who's Who mission to uplift, highlight and document the achievements of African Americans. It is my hope that our readers are inspired to share this valuable information, especially with our youth – the next generation of civil rights activists, global leaders, entrepreneurs, pastors, educators and parents.

Without the support of our sponsors and advertisers this publication would not have been possible. Through your support, you have helped us create a piece of history. On behalf of Who's Who Publishing, we thank you.

Sincerely,

Hiram E. Jackson

Over 105 Years of Caring for Our Communities

For more than 105 years, our commitment and involvement in the community has been recognized as an important part of the way we do business. Each day we strive to earn, build and maintain a positive relationship of trust with the millions of customers we serve in more than 150 communities throughout Texas and Mexico. In this spirit, we have contributed five percent of our pre-tax earnings to public and charitable programs since the 1930s, and remain one of the few companies in the nation to give at such a level. To invest in our communities, we support efforts to make a positive impact in the following areas:

Hunger Prevention

Established in 1982, the H-E-B Food Bank Assistance Program has donated more than 26 million pounds of food annually to 16 food banks to support their fight against hunger and malnutrition. The Feast of Sharing dinners are the highlight of our year-round effort to combat hunger. H-E-B serves free holiday meals to more than 250,000 people in 30 communities throughout Texas and Mexico.

Education

As a major supporter of public education, H-E-B contributes more than $7.9 million annually to education-related programs. Additionally, we have established the H-E-B Excellence in Education Awards, the H-E-B Classroom Champions program, and the H-E-B Fund for Teacher Excellence.

Health and Wellness

H-E-B is committed to the well-being of Texans and is a strong supporter of health and wellness initiatives across the state. Our initiatives drive awareness and behavior change, resulting in improved nutrition and increased physical activity for children and their families.

Environment

H-E-B is committed to environmental efforts. We have launched programs like the H-E-B School Recycling Program. Additionally, H-E-B was the first retailer in Texas to offer E-85 fuel at five of its fuel stations.

Supplier Diversity

At H-E-B, we value our partnerships with women and minority suppliers. Through their contributions, we better understand the needs of our customers and add to the growth of our company and the communities we serve.

Diversity

At H-E-B, we uphold the Bold Promise that "each and every person counts" by meeting the diverse needs of our customers, insuring our Partners reflect the communities we serve, and creating a culture of diversity and inclusion within our work environment.

Disaster Relief

H-E-B is a major contributor to emergency relief efforts during natural disasters through the deployment of the H-E-B Eddie Garcia Mobile Kitchen and Spirit of H-E-B trailer. These vehicles provide on-site food preparation and transport much needed supplies to communities in crisis.

Volunteerism

H-E-B encourages a strong spirit of volunteerism in its Partners. Everyday, hundreds of Partners from all areas of the company dedicate their time and energy to support our outreach efforts.

For more information about H-E-B's Spirit of Giving, visit www.heb.com.

IMPACT
STRATEGIES CONSULTANTS

Our focus is to provide customized, value-added solutions through innovative and strategic methods to positively IMPACT our client's bottom line.

Core Business Areas:
- » Business Development
- » Project Management
- » Diversity Marketing
- » Meeting and Special Event Planning
- » Workforce Development

Certifications:
- » Houston Minority Supplier Development Council (MBE)
- » State of Texas – Historically Underutilized Business (HUB)
- » Women Business Enterprise Alliance (WBE)
- » City of Houston (MBE/WBE)

For more information contact:
Customerservice@Impact06.com

www.Impact06.com

CHANGING LIVES & *Creating*
BRIGHT FUTURES
H O U S T O N   A R E A   U R B A N   L E A G U E

43rd Annual Equal Opportunity Day Gala
Saturday, June 25, 2011 ✳ Hilton Americas Hotel

HONORARY CHAIR

Mr. David Mendez
JPMorgan Chase Bank

HONOREES

Occidental Petroleum *Gerald Hines Corporate Award*
Fleishman Hillard *Whitney M. Young Humanitarian Award*
BP *Heritage Award*
COMCAST *Quentin Mease Community Service Award*
ConocoPhillips Black Employees Network *Margurite Ross Barnett Leadership Award*

For more information go to
www.haul.org or call (713) 393-8765

Houston Area Urban League | *Empowering Communities.*
Changing Lives.

United Way
United Way of Greater Houston

A United Way Agency affiliated
with the National Urban League

Howard E. Jefferson
CHAIRMAN

Mark A. Williams
PRESIDENT/CEO

PROTECTORS
INSURANCE & FINANCIAL SERVICES LLC.

Protecting Your Interest... That's Our Policy!

AS AN INDEPENDENT AGENCY WE OFFER THE FOLLOWING COVERAGE:

Commercial Property • Commercial Auto • General Liability • Business Insurance

Worker's Compensation • Auto • Home • Life and Health • Retirement

Medicare Supplement • Medicare Advantage

We Proudly Represent...

and many more...

National Representation • Your Local Houston Office

1177 WEST LOOP SOUTH, STE. 625 | HOUSTON, TEXAS 77027 | OFFICE: 713-660-8899 | FAX: 713-660-9977

www.protectorsinsurance.com

CENTER YOURSELF

The biggest hotel in Houston is hard to ignore.

The Hilton Americas-Houston is not only within walking distance to all the upscale dining, shopping and entertainment options downtown Houston has to offer, it is also conveniently connected to the convention center.

- *Over 1,200 rooms*
- *91,500 square feet of meeting space*
- *Direct skywalk connection to the Convention Center*
- *Across from Discovery Green Park*

Hilton
Americas-Houston

AmericasHouston.Hilton.com
877.432.3600

Criteria for Inclusion

Who's Who In Black Houston® is an opportunity for us to afford a measure of recognition to the men and women who have made their mark in their specific occupations, professions, or in service to others in the Houston community.

A sincere effort was made to include those whose positions or accomplishments in their chosen fields are significant and whose contributions to community affairs, whether citywide or on the neighborhood level, have improved the quality of life for all of us.

The names of those brief biographies included in this edition were compiled from customary sources of information. Lists of a wide variety were consulted and every effort was made to reach all whose stature or civic activities merited their inclusion.

In today's mobile society, no such publication could ever claim to be complete; some who should be included could not be reached or chose not to respond, and for that we offer our apologies. Constraints of time, space and awareness are thus responsible for other omissions, and not a lack of good intentions on the part of the publisher. Our goal was to document the accomplishments of many people from various occupational disciplines.

An invitation to participate in the publication was extended at the discretion of the publisher. Biographies were invited to contribute personal and professional data, with only the information freely submitted to be included. The editors have made a sincere effort to present an accurate distillation of the data, and to catch errors whenever possible. However, the publisher cannot assume any responsibility for the accuracy of the information submitted.

There was no charge for inclusion in this publication and inclusion was not guaranteed; an annual update is planned. Comments and other concerns should be addressed to:

Who's Who Publishing Co.
3700 Corporate Drive, Suite 110
Columbus, Ohio 43231
Phone: (614) 481-7300

www.whoswhopublishing.com

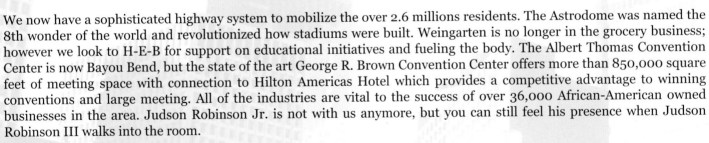

Houston's
VERNITA HARRIS
ASSOCIATE PUBLISHER

As a native Houstonian, it gives me great pride to pick up the torch and move forward with the fifth edition of *Who's Who in Black Houston*®. Our forefathers' vision for us was limited to the cotton fields and incorporated legalized illiteracy. As the daughter of two former cotton pickers and avid readers, I am amazed of the changes that I have witnessed in the past half century in Houston and America.

Houston and I grew up together. The Colt 45s played outside before there was an Astrodome or Houston Astros. The Houston ROCKETS' home was Hofhienz Pavilion and they were support by Weingarten Grocery as they waited on the completion of the Summit in 1975. The Albert Thomas Convention Center played host to conventions and major acts that came through the city. I met Judson Robinson Jr. in my neighborhood working on a community project and recalled him from television as the new and first black city councilman making a difference and empowering everyone he met. His presence filled the room.

This year there is a large migration to Houston by many who seek to fulfill the American dream, escape harsh winters and the recession. Only second to New York City as home of Fortune 500 companies, we have a broad industrial base. We are home to the largest medical center in the world and the most advance medical care possible within a 20-minute drive. The Johnson Space Center offers mission control, training and planning for the space program; it is unparalleled in sparking the interest in science for our children and future astronauts.

We now have a sophisticated highway system to mobilize the over 2.6 millions residents. The Astrodome was named the 8th wonder of the world and revolutionized how stadiums were built. Weingarten is no longer in the grocery business; however we look to H-E-B for support on educational initiatives and fueling the body. The Albert Thomas Convention Center is now Bayou Bend, but the state of the art George R. Brown Convention Center offers more than 850,000 square feet of meeting space with connection to Hilton Americas Hotel which provides a competitive advantage to winning conventions and large meeting. All of the industries are vital to the success of over 36,000 African-American owned businesses in the area. Judson Robinson Jr. is not with us anymore, but you can still feel his presence when Judson Robinson III walks into the room.

This history book documents the accomplishments of *Who's Who in Black Houston*®, those who bring out the best in our community to improve our city. Please take the time to read the stories of the individuals in this book. Their contributions vary across disciplines. As we enjoy the diverse multicultural city we live in, it is my sincere hope this book will inspire children of all races while providing a roadmap to success. A special thanks to Reliant Energy for ensuring that every child in the Houston Independent School District has access to the book through their school library.

My successes, failures, experiences and education build my character daily and I am sustained by my faith. I was blessed to have a family that encouraged God and education throughout my entire life. To my family, friends, Prairie View A&M University and Wheeler Avenue Baptist Church, you are my foundation in which I continue to grow. I appreciate your love and support and this book is dedicated to you.

Vernita Harris

Vernita B. Harris
Associate Publisher

Houston's CORPORATE SPOTLIGHT

INTEREST

LIMELIGHT

ATTENTION

PROMINENCE

HIGHLIGHT

CELEBRATE

HEADLINE

FOCUS

RECOGNITION

FEDERAL RESERVE BANK OF DALLAS · HOUSTON BRANCH

Donald Bowers

Assistant Vice President
Houston Branch
Federal Reserve Bank of Dallas

Erika D. Gloyd

Public Relations Representative
Houston Branch
Federal Reserve Bank of Dallas

Donald Bowers, a native Houstonian, received a bachelor's degree from Rice University in 1991. In 2004 he was promoted to assistant vice president of the Federal Reserve Bank of Dallas, Houston Branch, and his responsibilities currently include the bank's human resources, public affairs, law enforcement and business continuity functions.

Donald and his wife, Shawn, are the proud parents of two outstanding young men. He is a Blue and Gold Recruiting Liaison for the Naval Academy, president of the local Naval Academy Parents Club and a member of the Texas 9th Congressional District Service Academies Selection Committee.

Donald has served on the boards of the Houston Area Urban League and Prairie View A&M College of Business. He is also active with the Greater Houston Partnership, the World Affairs Council of Houston, Youth About Business, the Discovery Youth Foundation and the Fifth Ward Church of Christ youth programs.

Donald earned a Master of Business Administration degree from Sam Houston State University with a concentration in banking and finance. He is a graduate of the United Way's Project Blueprint Leadership Program and a member of the Rice University Alumni Board.

Erika D. Gloyd is public relations representative for the Federal Reserve Bank of Dallas, Houston Branch. She produces bank publications and assists with community programs and events. Erika is a member of the leadership team for Money Week Houston, the Prairie View Communi-versity Advisory Board and a liaison with Bank on Houston. She is an active volunteer teacher with Junior Achievement and a proud member of Alpha Kappa Alpha Sorority, Inc. She also serves on the Houston Branch's United Way committee.

Erika received a Bachelor of Business Administration degree from Sam Houston State University and a master's degree in journalism from the University of Illinois. She also holds a teaching certificate for grades 4 through 8.

A native of Houston, Texas, Erika is the wife of Roosevelt Gloyd III and the proud mother of two daughters, Riya and Aubrey.

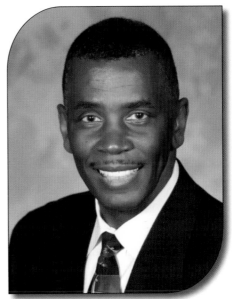

Angela R. Gobert-Conway

District Recruiter & Relocation Coordinator
Houston Branch
Federal Reserve Bank of Dallas

Oscar Greenleaf

Assistant Chief of Police
Houston Branch
Federal Reserve Bank of Dallas

With more than nine years experience in human resources, Angela Gobert-Conway currently serves as a recruiter for the Houston and Dallas offices of the Federal Reserve Bank of Dallas. She is also responsible for coordinating the relocation program for the Dallas Federal Reserve District, which includes the bank's headquarters in Dallas, as well as the branches in El Paso, Houston and San Antonio. In addition to her recruiting and relocation responsibilities, she is the system administrator for the district's recruiting software and coordinates the intern program for the Houston Branch.

For the past 11 years, Angela has been an active member of Alpha Kappa Alpha Sorority, Inc., where she has served in several leadership capacities. She holds a Bachelors of Business Administration degree in finance, cum laude, from Texas Southern University and a Master of Business Administration degree in finance from the University of St. Thomas. She is also a certified human resources professional.

Angela is the wife of Bo Conway and the proud mother of one daughter, Camryn.

As assistant chief of police for the Federal Reserve's Houston facility, Oscar Greenleaf is responsible for administrative and operational oversight of police operations and training. He holds certifications in law enforcement, emergency management and safety management and assumes collateral duties in safety management, recruitment, equal opportunity and business continuity. Greenleaf also held similar accountable positions with the U.S. Army, attaining the rank of colonel.

Greenleaf currently serves on the Bush Cares Project Board of Directors and the Emergency Preparedness Committee of the Federal Executive Board. He is an active member of the Association of Contingency Planners, Council on Occupational Safety and Health, Greater Houston Partnership and Money Week Houston.

A graduate of the U.S. Army War College and the Command and General Staff College, Greenleaf holds a bachelor's degree from Prairie View A&M University and a master's degree from the U.S. Army War College. Greenleaf is a certified safety and health official, Department of Labor OSHA outreach instructor, trained mediator and continuity of operations manager.

CORPORATE SPOTLIGHT

Jackie Hoyer

Senior Community Development Advisor
Houston Branch
Federal Reserve Bank of Dallas

Shawn Rose

Procurement Sourcing Coordinator
Houston Branch
Federal Reserve Bank of Dallas

As senior community development advisor for the Federal Reserve Bank of Dallas, Jackie Hoyer serves as a liaison between the Federal Reserve and Houston-area financial institutions, sharing information on personal financial education, community and economic development issues, and the Community Reinvestment Act. She has held similar positions with Bank of America and Washington Mutual. Hoyer has worked on affordable housing initiatives, foreclosure prevention initiatives, down payment assistance programs and homebuyer counseling programs.

She currently serves on the boards of the Credit Coalition of Houston as vice president and Houston Habitat for Humanity as vice chair. Additionally, she serves in an advisory capacity for Texas Southern University's Jesse H. Jones School of Business Advisory Council and Prairie View A&M University's Graduate School of Community Development Advisory Committee. She is a fellow in the 26th class of the American Leadership Forum, Houston/Gulf Coast Chapter, and a member of the Fall 2010 class of the Center for Houston's Future.

Hoyer is a licensed Texas real estate agent, holds a leadership certificate from Rice University's Jesse H. Jones Graduate School of Management and has a bachelor's degree from Ohio Wesleyan University.

Shawn Rose is the procurement sourcing coordinator for the Federal Reserve Bank located in Houston. Shawn coordinates the procurement activities for the Federal Reserve Bank Branches in El Paso and San Antonio as well as its headquarters in Dallas. She is the district's liaison to the Federal Reserve System's National Procurement Office. In addition to her procurement responsibilities, she is the supplier diversity coordinator for the Dallas district.

Shawn is active in the Bay Area Chapter of the National Association of Purchasing Managers, the Institute for Supply Management, the National Minority Supplier Development Council and the Houston Minority Supplier Development Council. She is also a committee member of the Greater Houston Partnership. She is a graduate of the United Way's Project Blueprint Leadership Program, has been a volunteer on the United Way Allocations Committee as well as serves as the treasurer of the Houston Branch United Way committee.

Shawn attended Sam Houston State University and the University of Houston. She received certifications in Purchasing and Supply Chain Management and Management and Leadership from the University of Houston Clear Lake.

Shawn and her husband are the proud parents of two sons.

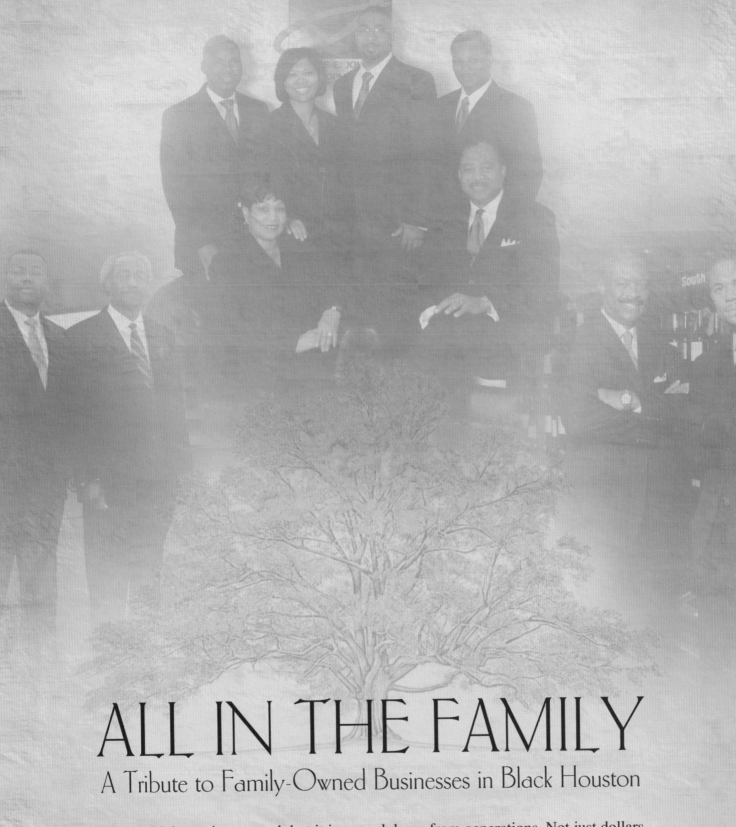

ALL IN THE FAMILY

A Tribute to Family-Owned Businesses in Black Houston

Wealth is not just earned, but it is passed down from generations. Not just dollars, but the wealth of knowledge, business savvy and thinking outside the box. The Johnson Family works collectively to make a house a home for families and businesses across the region. The Lewis Family believes that the entrepreneurial spirit is in their DNA. The Luckett's are proof that success can be as sweet as fine wine. These stories highlight three families in Houston who have built a legacy of wealth that enhance their communities and set an example of generational pride.

The Real Estate Dream Team

The Johnson Family
George E. Johnson Development, Inc.

By Donald James

The Johnsons have made George E. Johnson Development, Inc. a successful family affair. Their dream of building a real estate enterprise is a direct result of their belief in faith, family and having a lot of fun along the way. At the business helm are George E. Johnson Jr. and his spouse, Thomasine Johnson. Started in 1974 as Johnson and Sons, the company included the Johnson's sons. At that time the boys were under the age of three and daughter, Courtney Johnson, had not yet been born.

Johnson Jr., who currently serves as president and principal-in-charge of the company, describes the business as a comprehensive real estate development entity that facilitates projects in residential and commercial real estate, real estate development, construction and interior designs. In the company's 36 years, it has amassed an incredible portfolio of services to include community development projects for social, government and for profit and nonprofit entities. Projects have included single-family homes, multifamily housing, retail and social and religious center developments. Since the company's inception, it has managed more than $1 billion in residential and commercial real estate projects.

Thomasine, a professional interior designer, oversees the company's construction interior design projects. Her keen eye for detail, coupled with a heart of gold to serve the less fortunate, has won the company several community service interior design awards.

Courtney Johnson Rose currently spearheads the company's residential and commercial real estate divisions. Like father, like daughter, she has risen to become of one Houston's most respected real estate executives.

The youngest of the Johnson siblings, Courtney appreciates the great real estate lessons that were taught by her mother and father. "As children, my brothers and I were always around the office just watching how our father and mother operated the business," she recalls. "We would go with our parents on real estate showings and really learned the fundamentals of the business. My siblings and I have been around the many facets of real estate for a long, long time." Perhaps Courtney's greatest honor came recently when she and her mother earned master degrees at the same time, which both have used in community development endeavors in relationship with the company.

Joining Courtney are siblings: George Johnson III (principal-in-charge of construction division); Coy Johnson (project manager); and Quincy (project manager) in the construction business. George Johnson III first became interested in construction when he was project manager overseeing the construction of homes and restoration following both Hurricanes Katrina and Ike. This project enabled him to pull from prior management experience in corporate America and an IT background to develop critical, first-time, data management systems.

The eldest sibling, Coy Johnson, recently joined the company and works as a project manager for the construction and community development divisions. Quincy Johnson pioneered the start of the siblings' involvement. He worked tirelessly as a project manager to help build the company.

Courtney's spouse, Teeba Rose, is also a part of the family business lending his expertise in marketing and publicity. Teeba's outreach efforts have been integral to the company packaging its services and gaining new business opportunities.

The coming together of this family in real estate was not just by chance; the elder Johnson had a master plan. "It was my vision and plan that at some point the children would unite as a family to fully run the business," recalls Johnson Jr. "To have it really happen has been a huge blessing. Four years after I started the company with my young sons, I purchased two Century 21 franchises, which primarily specialized in residential real estate deals. In 1995 we changed the company's name to George E. Johnson Development, Inc. to represent the full scope of what we were doing, and to reflect the inclusion of the entire family in the business."

While the company is primarily operated by family, Johnson Jr. quickly points out that there are many non-family professionals that make valuable contributions to the success of the company's many projects. "We view everyone that works with us as part of our family, and it is important that we are inclusive of everybody's talents and skill sets," he explains. "We can only go so far as a business with just family members; so we value the contributions of our extended family team members to the success that's been achieved and to where we are going in the future."

While the company has worked on many real estate and development projects in Houston and throughout Texas over the years, Johnson Jr. points to the ongoing Pointe 2.3.4. as the most comprehensive project the company has been involved in to date. Under the leadership of Pastor KirbyJohn Caldwell and the Windsor Village United Methodist Church family, this faith-based project is now in its final completion phase. This 234-acre development consist of 462 single family residences, a 124-unit senior living facility, commercial businesses, including Walgreens, CVS, McDonald's, Taco Bell, a medical center with a Texas Children's Clinic, an elementary school, a YMCA, a 200,000 sq. ft. community center called the Kingdom Builders Center and more.

The Johnson Family

According to the Johnsons, the economic impact of this massive project that is 90 percent complete is in excess of $180 million. "We have a huge interest in working with faith-based organizations, which is a major part of our nonprofit portfolio," reveals Johnson Jr. "We feel that the Pointe 2.3.4. development is the model for Community Development and Revitalization in the country."

After 36 years in the real estate business, the Johnsons show no sign of slowing down. "Life is good," says Johnson Jr. "We are appreciative of having an opportunity to work and be successful as a family. Together, we bring new ideas, new life and new technological knowledge to the business. It's been a tremendous blessing."

Preparation Meets Opportunity

Sherman Lewis, Sherman Lewis III, Gena Lewis Singleton
The Lewis Group

By Terreece M. Clarke

"The family that prays together, stays together." In Houston - the family that prays, plays and develops multi-million dollar enterprises, stays together. Mutual trust, respect, love, and support, combined with tremendous individual achievement, has allowed the family to turn The Lewis Group LLP (TLG) into one of the largest minority owned companies in the Houston area.

The Lewis family legacy began with patriarch Sherman L. Lewis who embodies his own mother's dream for her children. Sherman remembers, while she only had an eighth grade education, his mother wanted and expected more for her children. Sherman spent the first eight years of his education in a two-room schoolhouse; by 1977 he had received a B.S. degree in agricultural economics from Langston University and his Masters degree in Public Administration from Harvard University's Kennedy School of Government.

Sherman and his wife Berniece, who is also an important part of their family's success, passed on their same education expectations to their children, Sherman Lewis III (known in the family as Trey) and Gena Lewis Singleton. Trey attended Virginia Tech and graduated with a Bachelor's degree in Economics with a concentration in finance and marketing. Gena graduated from Washington University with a degree in sociology, psychology and later, a law degree.

"Education is the great equalizer," Sherman said. "It levels the playing field so you can compete and provide for your family, children and grandchildren."

Building a multigenerational foundation for the family is what brought the Lewis' together in business.

Gena was the catalyst for the venture. She alerted her brother, Trey, to an opportunity with Shell Oil Company to become a multi-site operator of convenience stores and gas stations. After undergoing a lengthy process, the family was approved and founded the business in 2003 by purchasing 11 convenience stores.

Within a short period of time, Shell recognized TLG for their superior operational and management skills and the group acquired 13 additional stations. In 2007, when Shell divested themselves of all their real estate holdings, the group purchased 10 of their station's real estate holdings and became wholesalers of Shell Oil products.

"It was the opportunity to think long term," Trey said. "It was a decision about multigenerational goals.

"We always talked about going into business together, to pool our resources and build wealth for our family," Sherman said.

While many warn against mixing business and blood, the Lewis family is an example of family business done right.

"We're a close knit family and it brought us closer together," Sherman said. "We realized the strengths and weaknesses we each had. We are more respectful of each other as individuals...We never argue over who gets what because it is well defined - written down. Gena and I have input into the decision making process, but there needs to be one person that makes the decision. Trey, the CEO makes the final decision. Being there day to day, he has a much broader scope on the business, we lean on him."

Trey remarked that the majority of what is made is invested back into the business as they focus on growth so there isn't anything to argue over anyway.

Sherman and Trey praised Gena for discovering the Shell opportunity and bringing the family together in Houston when they previously had been in different states around the country. She used her contacts and knowledge of the city to make it home for her brother and father.

What the family has been able to do in a few short years is phenomenal and it speaks to the individual achievements and experience each member brought to the group.

"We work hard to take advantage of opportunities when they come," Trey said. "My father always taught me 'luck is where preparation meets opportunity.'"

"Doing all those things; preparing, working hard, getting an education, trusting in God – that's first – staying the course...that's what it takes," Sherman said.

In August of 2009, opportunity knocked again at The Lewis Group's door and Trey diversified the company's holdings by purchasing 11 Jack in the Box restaurants and adding an additional 10 sites in 2010. The company also acquired popular downtown Houston restaurant CABO Mix-Mex Grill in 2008. The company has grown from 55 employees with $6 million in annual revenues to over 600 employees with $100 million in revenues.

Sherman Lewis III and his father, Sherman Lewis

Preparation for the future began with Sherman's successful military career and his work for the United States Department of Agriculture in Oklahoma where he held several high level positions including Assistant Administrator for the Midwest. As Assistant Administrator, he was responsible for more than 2000 employees in 12 states and a $150 million dollar budget. He received numerous awards and recognitions including a Superior Service award for his management skills and ability to motivate employees.

When Lewis retired, he worked with Langston University as assistant administrator for Extension and Outreach. Tasked with reaching out to small, minority business owners, small-underserved farmers, rural communities and 4 H youth programs, he received the U.S. Department of Commerce award for Outstanding Commitment to Excellence.

Trey prepared his future by starting his first business in college. He developed a computer-training program for incoming freshman who lacked comprehensive computer skills. An overwhelming success, he trained over 600 incoming freshman. After graduation, he worked with Citicorp in both Washington D.C. and New York City and later with Apple Computer as the southeast sales manager for Fortune 500 corporate accounts.

During the same time period, he began to invest in the rapidly growing real estate market in Northern Virginia accumulating properties worth over $2.5 million dollars. He also founded E-Agent, a technology company that provided leads to real estate agents. It grew from no revenue to $1.5 million in less than a year. Recognizing the real estate bubble, Trey sold his properties and soon The Lewis Group was born.

Gena, who set the ball in motion for the creation of the Lewis Group, has been serving law students at the South Texas College of Law since 1991. Currently, she is the Assistant Dean of Student Academic Affairs and is licensed to practice law in the state of Illinois. She is married to Eric L. Singleton, also a lawyer and has one stepson, Chevon and one daughter, Erica.

The Lewis family is not solely focused on personal and business success. They believe in giving back to the community that has given them so much. In fact, their community involvement is as much a part of their plan for the Lewis legacy as providing security for future Lewis generations.

"We want to pass it on, to continue to work hard and reinvest and promote job opportunities for the Houston community." Sherman said.

They are active in the Urban League, the NAACP, Houston Citizens Chamber of Commerce, C-Stem and the Greater Houston Partnership as well as other local organizations and several Historically Black Colleges, including Lewis' alma mater Langston University. Trey also mentors young men and women about building their own businesses.

"I want them to know that we as a community need to focus on long term thinking – planning and wealth creation. Saving what you can now so you can do more tomorrow," Trey said. "I tell them you don't achieve goals overnight and to be prepared for when that window of opportunity opens up. I love talking with them. They need to know it's possible to be an entrepreneur."

Entrepreneurial Connoisseurs
Wayne M. Luckett, Warren B. Luckett
Branwar Wine Distributing Company

By Damon Autry

It's a beverage that some experts say dates back as far as 6000 B.C. It's made of fermented grapes and comes in a variety of colors and flavors. It has names such as cabernet sauvignon, merlot and pinot noir; chardonnay, riesling and sauvignon blanc. This is wine, and Americans have enjoyed its pleasures for centuries. Wayne M. Luckett, however, wasn't one of them—at least not initially. It was much later in life that Wayne developed a liking for the beverage that some say was first developed around the Caspian Sea and in Mesopotamia, which is near present-day Iran.

Wayne worked for more than 30 years before retiring as a telecommunications executive. His responsibilities called for him to travel to various destinations around the globe, including a five-year stint in Johannesburg, South Africa. It was here that Wayne, much to his surprise, gained an appreciation for South African wine. Realizing that South Africans routinely drank wine with dinner, he joined in on the tradition and eventually found himself interested in bringing back as many bottles as he could upon his return to the United States. "The quality of South African wine is extraordinary," he says. "So I brought back about 200 bottles with me thinking that would last about two years. Well, it lasted all of about six months."

Wayne then contacted a colleague who remained in South Africa to have him ship more wine his way. His friend, Ron Gault, and his wife, Charlayne Hunter-Gault, quickly shared with Wayne that they had started a wine label and that Wayne should use his love, appreciation and knowledge of wine and serve as a broker for South African wine into the United States. Heeding this advice, Wayne created Branwar International as a brokerage company. Ironically, Branwar International was not Wayne's first foray into the realm of entrepreneurship. That occurred several decades earlier when at 12 years old, he teamed with his dad on a paper route. Using his bike and relying on his dad to use his pick-up truck to supplement the youngster's bourgeoning entrepreneurial endeavor, Wayne's first business venture allowed him to fully understand what it meant when his dad spoke endlessly about doing the best you can do regardless of the kind of job you have. Several years later, the father and son tandem developed a landscaping business that they worked on Saturdays. "We worked as a team and split the profits down the middle," he recalls. "My dad instilled in my younger sister and me a strong work ethic and discipline. I used what my dad taught us – his support, his encouragement – and graduated from college. I became the first to graduate from college in my family, too."

Wayne earned a bachelor's degree in mathematics from the University of Houston and began working for SBC immediately after college. In addition to his responsibilities abroad, some of his domestic duties involved working with NASA, where he designed satellite-to-ground circuitry for various Apollo space missions. A one-year hiatus followed his retirement before dusting off his entrepreneurial skill set with Branwar International.

Desiring a bigger stake in the wine business, Wayne expanded his brokerage business and became a distributor, thus launching Branwar Wine Distributing Company in July 2010. Not only does Wayne distribute Ron and Charlayne's wine, but he also serves as the wholesale distributor for other leading South African labels. "South Africa has been making wine for many, many years, and folks in the U.S. didn't really know about it," he admits. "South African wine is one of the best-kept secrets in the world, so we're happy to introduce these wines to the clientele in the U.S., specifically here in Texas." Wayne's view about the products' virtues were affirmed when person after person tried the wine and instantly beamed with delight afterwards. "That's when I fully realized that I was onto something, and that's also when I realized that quality sells itself."

The legacy of a father/son partnership that began with Wayne and his dad has now expanded to the next generation. Warren, the oldest of Wayne's sons, joined his dad in the family's wine distributing business in 2009. Like his dad, Warren exhibited entrepreneurial traits early on in life. "I remember selling finger paintings when I was a kid," Warren says. "I've also known since the first grade that I wanted to be the CEO of a company. Those were the first big words I learned as a kid: chief executive officer. What better way to become a chief

Wayne M. Luckett and his son, Warren Luckett

executive officer than by running a family business?"

Warren, the company's vice president of marketing and sales, graduated from Morehouse College with a degree in finance. He worked on Wall Street as a trader for two years at Morgan Stanley before returning home to help run the family business. Wayne enjoys the opportunity to grow a business with his son. "It's great," he says of the teamwork he and Warren have. "Where once the relationship was more like father and son, it's now more like business partners. We toss ideas around and I take to heart a lot of his opinions. I feel proud as a father when I see him step up and do things that continue to make our company successful." The duo looks at each other's strengths and realizes the partnership is a good match. Wayne's mathematical background and its inherent methodical and analytical principles coupled with Warren's finance background, youth, energy and reliance on fresh ideas make for a practical micro-macro venture.

When quizzed about the reasons behind starting a business after a highly successful career in the telecommunications industry, Wayne gives a very pragmatic answer. "I love owning my own business," he says matter-of-factly. "I want to put in a lot of hard work and see a successful company built from scratch. That brings me a lot of satisfaction."

Branwar Wine currently has seven labels and 12 wines with plans of doubling those figures soon. The company's portfolio consists of several varieties, including Beyerskloof Pinotage, Blouvlei Red Blend, Blouvlei Sauvignon Blanc, Blouvlei Klassique, Doolhof Merlot, Doolhof Cabernet Sauvignon, Epicurean Red Blend, Passages Chardonnay, Passages Merlot and Passages Blend. These wines are sold in high-end restaurants, wine bars and retail stores, and both Wayne and Warren are pleased with the market penetration so far, although plans remain in place for a broader reach. Some of the company's immediate goals include increasing revenue and expanding beyond Texas; some of its long-term goals center on continuing to make sound management decisions and having the Branwar Wine Distributing Company name forever synonymous with high-quality products. They're also looking to incorporate more wines from other countries into their portfolio, including Portugal, Spain, Italy and Australia.

The wine business is a highly competitive, multilayered industry that could completely engulf the unprepared. That's why Wayne and Warren have immersed themselves and become intimately knowledgeable about every conceivable aspect of the business. Everything from knowing what to look for when visiting the vineyards and wine makers in South Africa, to knowing what products the U.S. consumer would enjoy, to knowing the procedures of U.S. Customs and the rules and regulations surrounding importing products. These and many other concepts must be second nature if success in the wine business is the goal. The wine distribution business hasn't traditionally been an industry that has attracted African Americans. There are only a handful in the U.S., a fact that often triggers interesting encounters when Wayne and Warren walk into a meeting. "They look at us and ask what company we work for," Wayne says. "Many people we meet with don't perceive us as owners of a distributing company. But we don't look at it as a color thing. We look at it as having the opportunity to go out and try to sell a product. We're confident that we can compete in this environment."

Beyond the love of the business, beyond the joy of knowing customers enjoy their products, beyond all the perks and prestige that come with business ownership, Wayne has an even bigger reason why he launched Branwar Wine Distributing Company. "I'm interested in leaving a legacy for my kids," he says. "Something I can help build and eventually pass down to them. That's extremely important to me." In fact, the name Branwar itself pays homage to his sons. It's a combination of Warren and younger son Brandon, who's currently pursuing a career as a dentist. The lofty expectations of his dad aren't lost on Warren. "My dad has instilled in my brother and me the same thing his dad instilled in him: no matter what you do, strive to be the best. That's what we're doing with our business."

Wayne is married to Patricia and is an active member in both the church and community. He serves on several boards, is a proud member of Kappa Alpha Psi Fraternity, Inc. and enjoys traveling and playing golf.

All photos by Ken Jones

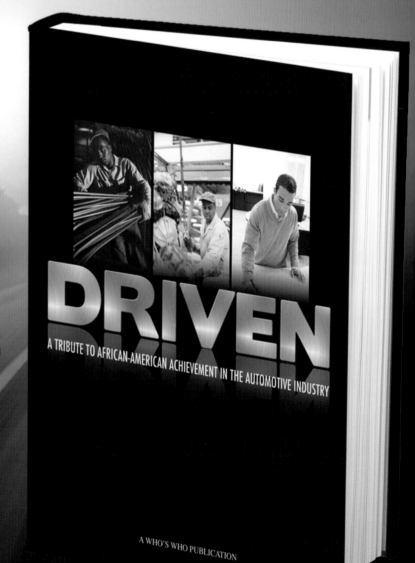

The Lewis Group LLP

The 600+ employees of The Lewis Group would like to congratulate all of the recipients of this years Who's Who in Black Houston. As an African American owned company we know the importance of strong mentors and leaders in our communities.

As Dr Martin Luther King said *"The first obligation of each generation is to invest in the next."*

13250 FM 1960 West | Houston TX 77065

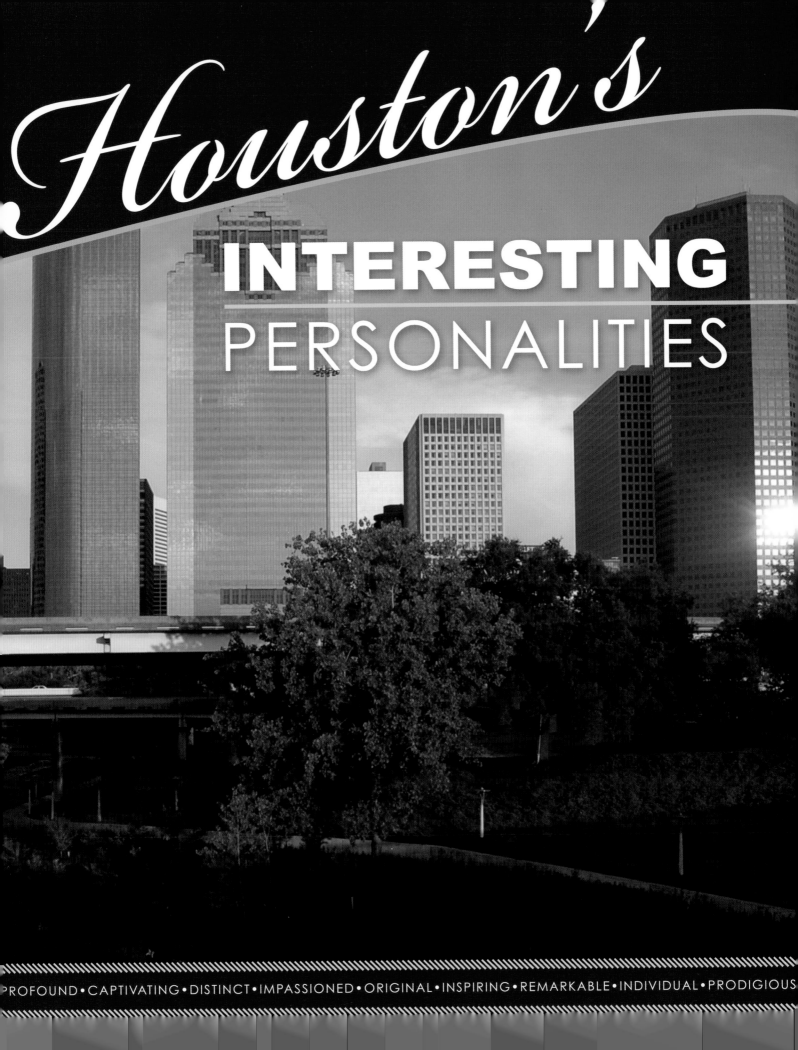

Houston's

INTERESTING

PERSONALITIES

PROFOUND · CAPTIVATING · DISTINCT · IMPASSIONED · ORIGINAL · INSPIRING · REMARKABLE · INDIVIDUAL · PRODIGIOUS

Photo by Ken Jones

NECESSITY IS THE MOTHER OF EDUCATION INVENTION

M. ANNETTE CLUFF

Founder & Superintendent,
The Varnett Public School

M. ANNETTE CLUFF

By Terreece M. Clarke

Education is the pathway to opportunity. In Annette Cluff's case, the education of her child paved the way for her to become the founder and superintendent of the largest charter school district for elementary education in Texas.

"My three-year-old son needed an educational environment that would provide an African-American perspective with strong emphasis on academic achievement," said Cluff. "We founded Varnett in 1984, acquired accreditation from the Texas Education Agency in 1985 and earned our charter in 1998. My son and daughter received a solid, well-rounded education at Varnett and they have a great understanding of multiculturalism."

Not many people can create a school from nothing, and Cluff credits this tremendous task and success with her business background.

"When I started my business, I ran out of money after having used my personal savings. After being turned down for a $25,000 loan by five banks, I was presented with a decision to continue or just throw in the towel and get a job back with Exxon," she said. "However, persistence paid off and I found a banker with whom I could negotiate and we worked out a satisfactory deal. The business world is a war of wills so what does not discourage you will make you stronger. Their denials strengthened me. Succeeding 'against all odds' became my destiny."

The school's East campus was named a 2010 National Blue Ribbon School, which was among only 14 charter schools in the country and the only charter school in Texas to earn the honor.

"Compromising or 'settling' in life is not an option," remarked Cluff. "I am driven to be the best I can be. My mission is to teach those values to our children."

Cluff's extensive resume is a result of her parents' lessons of hard work and high expectations.

"Both of my parents finished high school but they wanted more for their children," she said. "They felt that education was the best hope for us to have a quality life and a future filled with more opportunities than they had experienced. Going to college wasn't an option; it was expected."

Living up to those expectations, Cluff earned a Bachelor of Science degree in mathematics and education from Fayetteville State University in North Carolina, a Master of Science degree in computer science from New York University and is completing her doctorate in Educational Administration at Texas Southern University.

Cluff's professional success and awards include, participation in the China Teacher program in Beijing, the "Check Point Charlie" German Teacher program, the 1996 and 1998 *African-American Business Achievement Pinnacle* award; the 1997 *Texas Leader in the 90s* award by the Texas A&M University's Memorial Student Center Black Awareness Committee; the 1998 *Emerging 10* award and the 1999 *Texas Leaders in the 90s Award*. Additionally she was named the 2001 honoree for *Outstanding Contributions in Education* given by the Houston chapter of the National Black MBA Association and the 2008 *Minority Achiever's Award* presented by the YMCA of Greater Houston. She also is a major contributor to the Smithsonian National Museum of African American History and Culture. However, her accomplishments are second only to her commitment to community service and education.

"Each new classroom presents an opportunity to be a positive influence in the lives of our children, and the work is never done."

Photo by Ken Jones

HOUSTON PROUD

SIDNEY EVANS II
Senior Advisor, Texas Business Affairs
Reliant Energy

SIDNEY EVANS II

By Donald James

Since moving to Houston from Phoenix, Arizona 36 years ago, Sidney Evans has considered himself to be 'Houston Proud.' In his professional endeavors, he has had the opportunity to work closely with many community and civic associations and organizations in the city of Houston, the state of Texas and across the United States.

Evans is currently a senior advisor in the business affairs department of Reliant Energy, a Houston-based company that provides electricity and energy services to residential and commercial customers in the United States. Evans' responsibilities are to assist Reliant Energy in strengthening its ties and relationships with civic, community and other stakeholders in Houston, and throughout the entire state. He interfaces with more than 75 chambers of commerce, community associations and other industry organizations on behalf of the company. "I love what I do because in most situations when I meet with associations and organizations, I am the face of Reliant Energy," says Evans, now in his 10th year with Reliant Energy. "Therefore, how I am perceived is reflective of how Reliant Energy is perceived and I love that."

Prior to his work with Reliant Energy, Evans served as president of the Galleria Chamber of Commerce, which encompassed the Galleria, Uptown and Greenway Plaza areas. If the combined populations of the areas were a city, it would equate to be the 13th largest municipality in America. During his three-year stint, his efforts expanded the organization to become the 8th largest chamber in the Gulf Region. Through his professional and business acumen, Evans secured major sponsorships that significantly increased the Galleria Chamber's annual budget.

Evans' outstanding performance at the Galleria Chamber of Commerce was to be expected when he took the job. He had previously served nine years as director of membership and visitor services for the Greater Houston Convention & Visitors Bureau. Based on his recruitment and retention of members, the bureau consistently ranked as one of the top 10 membership programs in the nation, generating well over $1 million in revenue. It was during his tenure with the bureau that Evans established his impactful presence amongst community and civic groups, and their respective leaders.

Evans' knack for business development, networking and empowering communities comes natural for the Houstonian. However, he credits his father, Sidney Sr., as a great teacher for demonstrating professionalism. A well-respect accountant in Texas, Evans' father was the first African American in Arizona to become a Certified Public Accountant (CPA). "He taught me how to dress, talk to people and carry myself professionally," Evans says. "He gave me the proper guidance in how to socially adapt in various settings in life. He is my most important mentor, although my mom Wilma and brother Tony have always been there too."

Following somewhat in his father's footsteps, Evans earned a bachelor's degree in business administration from Stephen F. Austin State University, with career objectives to make bold strides in business environments. Following graduation, Evans returned to Houston to begin his professional career.

Although Evans, through his job, interfaces with 75 civic and community organizations, he is committed to personally working with several nonprofit entities, inclusive of board positions with the American Diabetes Association (Houston), Crime Stoppers of Houston, Houston Intercontinental Chamber of Commerce, and the North Houston Economic Development Council. Evans is the proud father of two children: Taylor and Trey.

Photo by Ken Jones

PRIDE, GRACE & EXCELLENCE

LAURENCE A. HUMPHRIES

Strategy & Planning Analyst
Exploration & Production Co.
Chevron Africa/Latin America

By Damon Autry

Laurence A. Humphries emanates an unmistakable conscientious spirit. It's in his demeanor. His talk. His actions. He exudes a sense of pride, both in his personal journey and the family from which he sprung. This is so because it is who he is; it's the way he was raised, thanks in large measure to the guiding grace of his nurturing mother and father who instilled in Laurence and his siblings a healthy sense of accurately appraised self-value. His father, Dr. Frederick S. Humphries Sr., the highly respected former president of Tennessee State and Florida A&M, often took Laurence out of school as a child so the youngster could accompany him on business trips. "I got a sense early on about what it meant to have responsibility and a commitment to achieving excellence," Laurence says.

Achievement has been one of Laurence's steady companions as an adult. He has been with Chevron since 2000 and serves as an analyst and advisor for the Africa and Latin America Exploration and Production Company where he focuses on Latin America. Since joining Chevron, he has served in both domestic and international roles in strategy and planning. He has worked in Africa, the Middle East, Europe and Latin America across Upstream, Midstream and the Downstream. He was appointed by the Obama Administration to serve on a Committee for Energy with the Department of Commerce. In this capacity he provides industry insights and perspective for the development of U.S. Multilateral and Bilateral Trade Agreements.

Growing up the son of a college president made it easy for Laurence to appreciate the excellent education that HBCU's provide. That convinced him that he needn't look anywhere but an HBCU for his educational pursuits. Consequently, Laurence applied to only one college out of high school – Morehouse College in Atlanta. He earned a bachelor's degree in marketing before later earning an MBA degree from Clark Atlanta University. "I believe it is important to set an example for our youth," he says. "That one can reach the highest levels of the American dream by attending these historically significant institutions. I hope my life serves as a model of this belief."

With a strong education behind him, Laurence aspired to work on Wall Street, but a trip with his father to Africa in 1991 triggered his desire to have a career where he could affect the economic and social uplifting of Africa. He eventually landed the job with Chevron, which he chose over a career on Wall Street because the company committed that he would have the opportunity to utilize his talents to conduct business in Africa. "The oil and energy industry is an exceptional industry," he says. "It has given me amazing opportunities to achieve my career aspirations. I'm in the indispensable industry that is only surpassed by NASA in the utilization of advanced technology."

Laurence resides in Houston and has two children, Laurence II and Dylan Gabrielle. He is a member of the World Affairs Council, American Association of Blacks in Energy, Society of Industry Leaders, Inaugural Ambassador, Millennium Network at The Clinton Foundation and former Committee Member, The Bush Clinton Coastal Recovery Fund.

LAURENCE A. HUMPHRIES

Photo by Ken Jones

IN THE FAST LANE

CARLA LANE

President & Chief Executive Officer
LaneStaffing

CARLA LANE

By Damon Autry

There comes a time in some people's professional lives when toiling for someone else at a 9-to-5 becomes a monotonous chore. But this is often the time when some search beyond themselves and their frustrations for something that is different and more rewarding; an opportunity that gives them the chance to start their own business and shape it to the styles and contours that fit them. Carla Lane was such a case.

Carla started with DiverseStaff, an employment-staffing firm in 2003 and moved her way up to senior vice president and chief operating officer. She fell in love with the business and the idea of helping people find work. However, she grew weary of where the company was headed and decided to purchase the company outright in 2007, renaming it LaneStaffing. From day one, she has had a simple business philosophy that gets more relevant every day; "It's people first, profits later," she says. "If we take care of people, the profits come. That's how the company has grown." LaneStaffing offers business stakeholders and hiring managers comprehensive solutions for all consulting, supplemental resources and recruitment needs. She further states, "We place everybody—from someone who will dig a ditch to someone who will create the IT infrastructure of a corporation."

Carla has nurtured her organization to become the largest minority woman-owned employment solution provider in the Southwest. She has also expanded the scope of LaneStaffing, increasing its client base of Fortune 100 and 200 clients, while becoming a leader in government contracting.

Carla has offices in Houston, Dallas, Ft. Worth, Port Arthur, Beaumont, and Galveston, Texas, as well as in Orlando, Florida.

A trait that is woven through every fiber of Carla's being is her sense of family. She grew up in a supportive two-parent household, with an older sister and younger brother. "Family is the basis of everything I do," she says. "Family gives me a sense of confidence because I know no matter what, I have people behind me and supporting me." For her entire life, Carla has remained close to her siblings. Part of that bond is due in some degree to growing up as the children of a preacher. Carla, whose dad leads Bibleway Bible Church in Dallas, says she and her siblings had to sometimes endure cruelty from others because "we were preacher's kids. But we stuck together through it all, and my sister and brother are my closest friends to this day. The way we look at it, it's us and then it's the rest of the world."

Carla has received numerous awards and acknowledgements for her outstanding business leadership. A Pinnacle Award in 2007, an Emerging Ten Award in 2008, a Distinguished Alumni Award from the University of Houston—the acknowledgements are plentiful. But there is one aspect of the accolades that gives Carla the most joy. "What makes my heart smile is when my daughter gets excited about something I've done, or an award that I've received," she says with a glow. "That shows her that she can do it too."

The University of Houston graduate and active member of Delta Sigma Theta Sorority, Inc., is married with two children.

Photo by Ken Jones

What Hard Work Looks Like

JACKIE LATHAN PHILLIPS

Vice President, Ethics & Compliance
Spectra Energy Corp

JACKIE LATHAN PHILLIPS

By Damon Autry

The root of Jackie Lathan Phillips' work ethic is easy to determine. She and her five siblings were reared in a two-parent household where resources were in short supply, but the surplus of love and discipline that poured from the family's home made up for the nonessential material goods the family went without. Jackie's dad worked at Holsum Bakery and would come home and play challenging word and math games with his kids, keeping their minds sharp and preparing them to mentally remain on their toes. Her mother worked at Louisiana State University (LSU) in the cafeteria, and it was always her mother's dream to see one of her kids attend the school. "Both of my parents were hard working people," Jackie recalls. "We had good examples of what hard work looked like."

Jackie began mirroring the hard work of her parents in earnest while attending LSU, essentially realizing the dream of her mother. "When we were kids, none of us wanted to go (to LSU) because our mother worked there," she says through a slight chuckle. "But I drew the short straw and ended up there, and it was one of the best things that ever happened to me." The absolute world of numbers and the challenges that are inherent in professions that center on them were what Jackie thirsted for. Consequently, she earned a degree in accounting, which, she says, gave her entrance into a business profession that would always be around. "I wasn't afraid of numbers. It's a challenging profession, but I get fulfillment from that challenge."

Jackie has been with Spectra Energy Corp since 1978 serving in roles of increasing responsibility. Indeed, her current role as vice president of ethics and compliance is demanding, but Jackie maintains a diligent focus on ensuring others maximize their talents – both in her professional and personal capacities. At work she helped found the company's Leadership Development Network (LDN). This employee-driven group was started as a result of concern expressed by some within the company over the retention of minority employees, as well as the relative lack of promotions of some minorities. LDN was developed as a way to address those concerns. The group has even had the opportunity to speak directly to Spectra's chief executive offcer to share its ideas and garner corporate support.

Personally, Jackie is heavily involved in the Ensemble Theatre as its board president, a nonprofit organization in existence since 1976 that seeks to preserve African-American expression, and to enlighten, entertain and enrich a diverse community. It is here where young people are encouraged to expand their horizons and pursue the arts. "Sometimes we think we participate (in a nonprofit) to help the organization, but what's surprising is how much the organization helps us. We get so much in return," she says. Timid and shy kids who enter the theatre program often transform into brilliant artists who spread their wings creatively and open themselves up to a world that was previously foreign to them. "It's amazing to see them grow like that," she says.

The little time Jackie gets is spent readtin. She says "I sometimes read as many as three books at a time." She enjoys hanging with her daughter Tracy and grandson Drew, all of whom are members of Windors Village United Methodist Church.

PUTTING THE HUMANITY IN HUMAN RESOURCES

OMAR CINQUE REID

Director, Human Resources Department
City of Houston

By Terreece M. Clarke

A human resource manager is *supposed* to live by the philosophy that people make the difference in an organization. There is, however, a drastic difference between knowing and living the example and Omar C. Reid is a person who lives the example. "Each day I try to make things better for the people I serve," Reid said. "I measure myself by 'Are things better? Or could they be better?'"

He follows three keys to success when working with others: trust, communication and perception is reality. "Trust is the basis of any successful relationship," Reid explains. "We were born with two ears and one mouth, which means we should listen more than we speak."

Reid has a goal – to change the culture of the HR department. Instead of a slow-moving, cumbersome bureaucracy, Reid is trying to boost the department's ability to be productive like the private sector. It's no easy task to manage and meet the needs of 22,000 city employees, but he is up for the challenge. He credits the lessons learned in previous positions for giving him the tools to affect change.

"In my former position at UPS, we were graded everyday," he says. "Everyday was a pass or fail and the failures taught me resiliency." Reid's extensive volunteer experience also prepared him for his current role. "I took unpaid positions within nonprofits and was able to hone my leadership skills," he clarifies. "Learning how to motivate volunteers taught me to become a better leader. When I saw a job that needed to be done I had to do it. I truly believe to whom much is given much is required."

Reid stresses the importance of education and mentorship in his rise to prominence.

"Getting an education was expected, but my parents were slick; they never pressured us, but we all understood," he said. "My father worked construction and took us with him all summer. It acted as a deterrent and a great learning experience. I cannot stress enough the importance of an education. Without it, it is impossible to compete."

Reid's list of achievements and community involvement is long and impressive. He has a bachelor's degree from the University of Houston and a master's degree from Texas Southern University. He has served as a leader in many community organizations including, the National Black Master of Business Administration, the Houston Black Leadership Conference, the United Way of Texas, the United Parcel Service's United Negro College Fund Walk-A-Thon and is the author of *The Traffic of Life: Characteristics of Effective Leadership*.

His commitment to serving his family, wife, Janice and daughter, Briana, and maintaining a healthy spiritual and physical lifestyle keeps him focused and humble.

"Bill Gates, Barack Obama and I all have one thing in common – we all have 24 hours to get things accomplished," he says. "How you utilize it reflects the balance in your life. Put God first. The things I have done would not be possible without God. I am blessed and it's great to be a blessing to others."

Photo by Ken Jones

SERIAL ENTREPRENEUR, SERIAL SUCCESS

MAURICE R. STONE

Chairman
National Clean Fuels Inc.

MAURICE R. STONE

By Terreece M. Clarke

When you are the child of a college president and everyone from activists and politicians, to sports legends and thought leaders take turns sitting at your childhood dinner table, you understand that there are high expectations for your life. Some children buckle and resent the pressure, but Maurice Stone embraced it.

"I had the best parents in the world," Stone said. "I sat at the dinner table listening to everything and was quizzed afterward on what was said."

His father Dr. Herman Stone, former president of Lane College in Jackson, Tennessee, was valedictorian of every class he attended. His mother, a schoolteacher, was salutorian of her college class and headed many social organizations. Stone credits his parent's achievements and deep Christian faith for his success.

"My father did everything excellently," he said. "He was the best example of a man I know." He also credits his spiritual belief in God. "I am where I am because of two fathers – one was the inspiration and one was the help. The Bible is the best business manual around. I am truly touched and blessed by God."

Stone's success is nothing short of amazing. A self-described serial entrepreneur, he has more than 30 years of extensive entrepreneurial and business management experience. His skills in business planning, financial planning, market analysis and media presentation make him a highly sought after executive.

He has served as chairman and chief executive officer of Intrepid Holdings and Cornerstone Services Group, Inc., where he was responsible for the management and supervision of the company, including their multi-site clinic services and pharmacy operations. He opened and operated 27 clinics, successfully acquired and consolidated the operations of nine pharmacies and executed the company's SEC reporting, Sarbanes-Oxley compliance and audit oversight.

Prior to his work with Intrepid Holdings and Cornerstone, he was chief executive officer of First Genesis, Inc. and an executive officer with both Intelligent Medicine, Inc. and Telemedicine Solutions International, Inc. He acted as a management consultant for Stone and Associates, general and limited partner of River City Broadcasting Ltd., senior sales manager at Digital Equipment Corporation and a marketing representative for IBM Corporation.

When asked about the adversity entrepreneurs have to overcome, Stone emphasized repeated effort. "If you don't try, you fail by default."

Stone's extensive resume led to his current position as chairman of National Clean Fuels, Inc., an emerging alternative energy company. He assists companies in commercializing and distributing cutting-edge alternative energy technologies and equipment domestically and internationally.

He serves on the board of directors of the National Black Chamber of Commerce and is the chairman of its Energy Committee. He is also a principal of Brown Shade Development, LLC, a company that provides business infrastructure, consulting and equity to emerging market companies.

"I'm a teacher by default. I like to inspire adults," he said. "Kids can't make changes and make an immediate impact but adults can. I want to inspire adults to take responsibility and change the way they view economic issues."

Stone is a loving husband to wife, Stephanie, a father to two daughters; Tiffany and Maury, one son; Stephen, and one grandson, Marquise.

Photo by Ken Jones

MAKING NUMBERS DANCE

TENE THOMAS

Partner
McConnell Jones Lanier & Murphy LLP

TENE THOMAS

By Terreece M. Clarke

When a child is gifted in dance, most dream of gracing the stages of famed theaters around the world. Indeed, Tene Thomas had an incredible opportunity to turn little girl dreams into adult reality when she was given the opportunity to study classical ballet under a Russian master. Fast forward several years and Tene Thomas is a partner in the largest minority-owned public accounting firm in Houston, Texas.

The young and driven professional realized the career length and opportunity of a ballet dancer didn't meet her high standards. She aspired for more. Behind Thomas' outgoing and magnetic personality is a woman with impeccable standards and a competitive spirit.

With an eye toward business, Thomas fell in love with accounting while in college at California Polytechnic University, Pomona. "During this time, I became controller of the Los Angeles African Marketplace overseeing a $2 million budget," explained Thomas "I realized that I really enjoyed what I was doing and was very good at it."

In a field where there aren't many women and even fewer minority women, Thomas has used self-discipline and thirst for challenge to quickly rise through the ranks at McConnell Jones Lanier & Murphy LLP (MJLM) to become the youngest partner in the firm. She describes herself as a 'lifer' in the field.

As partner of the Tax Department at MJLM, she is responsible for the organization's strategic growth initiatives and ensuring technical accuracy and quality control. She is also charged with providing leadership and mentoring to the firm's tax staff and leads the firm's small business solutions division where she works directly with entrepreneurs and small business owners.

"I embrace the responsibility to be a role model," she said. "I have made being a CPA a lifetime commitment, while the pressure causes most people to jump ship in two years. There's always a challenge. You're selling your knowledge, you're selling your time and because the laws are constantly changing, you have to stay on top of things. It's a unique opportunity to help clients and be that trusted advisor."

Thomas has set out to change the younger generation's perception of the 'typical CPA.' She has partnered with the NABA and Howard University to attract high school students to the accounting field.

"I'm very excited," Thomas said. "It's a chance to show them someone who looks like them who is not only in the field, but is at the table, in the boardroom, making the decisions."

With over 16 years of technical public accounting experience, Thomas uses her knowledge to help nonprofit organizations like the National Kidney Foundation of Southeast Texas, who need professional advice but lack resources.

Thomas has been a weekly business contributor on CNN's 650 AM talk radio program The Price of Business. She has been featured several times in the national trade magazine *Accounting Today* and is an active member of the Texas Society of CPA's and the American Institute of Public Accountants.

CHANGE AGENT FOR EXCELLENCE

LATOYA L. WALL

Founder & President
The Bulsard Group, LLC

LATOYA L. WALL

By Donald James

Latoya L. Wall is always in pursuit of excellence, a goal that she is accustomed to reaching. As the founder and president of The Bulsard Group LLC, Wall's company focuses on partnering with clients to facilitate operational excellence in such areas as business development, intellectual property and licensing, human resources, supply chain strategies and information technology. To achieve such goals and objectives, Wall operates as one of only a few African-American women in the United States to hold certification as both a Master Black Belt and Lean Six Sigma facilitator. This global certification places her in the higher echelon of executives qualified to lead teams of other top executives in planning, creating and facilitating strategies to improve every sector of a company. She has also developed and instructed training courses for Six Sigma Black Belts focusing on Lean Six Sigma basics. "We partner with companies to make sure that their operations are running in a fast but lean and efficient manner," Wall explains. "We remove all waste and rework steps that bring about value and accelerated growth."

The Bulsard Group's clients include such companies as Chevron and Raytheon. The company also has clients in the medical and aerospace industries respectively, and is expanding. Based in Houston, Texas, The Bulsard Group services clients in New Orleans, Chicago, San Francisco and Bakersfield, California.

Prior to starting The Bulsard Group, Wall worked as a design engineer and mechanical engineer for Raytheon in Boston. Wanting to return South, Wall moved to Houston where she began working for Chevron. While happily employed, she knew there was something else designed for her destiny. "I always had this entrepreneurial spirit within me," says the New Orleans native. "I just knew that it was time to venture out on my own. So I took a risk and started my own company here in Houston."

Wall was acutely aware that the industry was – and still is – dominated by white males. However, being the only black female was not a new experience for her. When she graduated from Louisiana State University with a bachelor's degree in mechanical engineering, she stood as the lone black female in her class. Wall was also one of only a few black female students in her graduating class at Boston University where she received a master's degree in project management. Based on her faith in God, and trusting in her God-given abilities, Wall unveiled The Bulsard Group, LLC in 2008.

In less than three years at the helm of The Bulsard Group, Wall has been recognized in the industry as a trailblazer and a true agent of change. *Black Enterprise* magazine recently featured her as one of the 40 Next young entrepreneurs to change the world. Additionally, *Essence Magazine* recently recognized her in its Power Issue as a woman who is doing great things in her industry and the community.

Always ready to give back through volunteerism, Wall works with several nonprofit organizations such as the Houston Citizens Chamber of Commerce, the Houston Minority Supplier Development Council, the Women Business Enterprise National Council and the International Society of Six Sigma Professionals. She also makes time to mentor young African-American women through her membership with the National Society of Black Engineers. However, there are two young women that Wall loves to mentor the most: daughters Kayla and Kaci.

Photo by Ken Jones

EXCELLENCE PERSONIFIED

STEFAN WILSON

Gulf South District President
UPS

STEFAN WILSON

By Donald James

As president of UPS's Gulf South District, Stefan Wilson has a massive job, and he loves it! Wilson oversees the company's district-wide operations (165,000 square miles) in Louisiana and southern Texas, which encompasses more than 17.1 million people and involves more than 11,000 employees. In addition, he coordinates UPS's heavy-frame aircraft logistics in the district, and tracks more than 600 tractor-trailers, 4,200 package cars, and 800,000 packages daily. Wilson knows the scope of his responsibility is enormous, but maintains control in an efficient and effective manner. "It's certainly a huge day-to-day challenge, but a challenge I dearly love," Wilson admits. "However, to successfully run a business like this it is important to bring about communication with those 11,000 employees in order to carry out the mission of the organization. So while much of it rides on my shoulders, I have a senior staff of 30 professionals who help make the overall business a success."

Wilson began his career at UPS in 1986 as a delivery driver in northeast Texas. Determined to excel in the company, he worked in various capacities to include human resources, engineering, small package operations and transportation. Prior to his current position as Gulf South District president, Wilson was president of South Florida and South New England districts, respectively, after serving as vice president of human resources for UPS Airlines. "My mission upon coming to UPS was to learn as much as I could," says Wilson. "Working in many of the key areas of the company has given me a sound platform in which to manage this business day-to-day." Since entering the executive ranks of the company, which has included six geographical moves, Wilson has taken advantage of ongoing executive leadership development programs.

Although Wilson calls his job a 24/7 commitment, he makes time to connect with many community and civic organizations and endeavors. Prior to moving to Houston in 2010, he was a loaned executive chairperson for the United Way Community Campaign in Hartford, Connecticut. He continues to be active in the National Urban League's Black Executive Exchange Program (BEEP), which provides mentorship opportunities for students attending Historically Black Colleges & Universities.

A native of Clinton, Louisiana, Wilson cites the support of the small town, and his parents' upbringing as the foundation for his success. Growing up, he was a standout football player in high school, which earned him a scholarship to Southern University. In college, he had thoughts of becoming a veterinarian but decided to major in economics. Soon after earning his bachelor's degree, he moved to Dallas, Texas, where he worked in human resources for a local company before being hired by UPS as a package driver.

Wilson knows that his journey to the top would not have been possible without the strong support of a loving family. He thanks Ursula, his wife of 25 years, for her support in standing with him in his many professional journeys. Wilson is also appreciative of the couple's two daughters' support: Stephanie, a student at Hampton University and Danielle, a student at Xavier University. "My family has made a tremendous amount of sacrifice for me to move to many places with the company," says Wilson. "I think our daughters must have gone to six or seven different schools because of the constant moves; but I know it has made them that much stronger. I thank them for their sacrifice."

Big Block

02

Block

02

A TEXAS LEGEND

RAY SEALS

Head Coach & Athletic Coordinator
Madison High School

RAY SEALS

By Donald James

For more than 45 years, Ray Seals has been one of the most successful high school football coaches in Texas – and the United States. Those who know Seals, and/or have played for him, describe the legendary coach as passionate and a great motivator of young people. While Seals is humbled when he hears such praises and accolades, there's no getting around the truth that he is a true winner.

Seals is currently the head football coach and athletic coordinator at Madison High School, where for a quarter of a century he has molded the inner city Houston school into a perennial football powerhouse. Prior to Madison, he was an accomplished head football coach at Milby High School. Other Houston schools where Seals have coached are: Houston Sterling High School (running back coach), Sam Houston High School (defensive coach) and M.C. Williams High School (offensive and defensive coach).

Over the last four decades the storied coach has received several dozen honors and awards as a testament to his living legacy, inclusive of garnering the first ever NFL Don Shula National Coach of the Year Award (2011); named NFL High School Coach of the Year (2009); received the Fellowship of Christian Athletes Coach of Influence Award (2008); recipient of the Houston Area Alliance of Black School Educators' Texas Legend Award (2008); inducted into the Texas High School Coaches Association Hall of Honor (2005); honored by the Houston Texans as a Texas Legend (2005); and named a Coach Who Makes a Difference in Sports and High School Football (1998). In addition, he has garnered Houston Coach of the Year Awards on 10 occasions, and has received the coveted Houston ISD/Houston Coaches Association Man of the Year Award five times. "The awards and honors are great," Seals humbly admits. "But for me, the real awards and honors are when the kids I've coached over the years come back and tell me that the things I taught them made a positive difference in their lives."

The line of former players who have come back to thank Seals has been long as he has coached more than 1,000 players, and prepared more than 225 football players to receive college scholarships across the United States. The fruit of Seals' labor can be found on many NFL rosters to include such players as Vince Young (Tennessee Titans), Tom Bruton (Baltimore Colts), Broderick Thomas (Tampa Bay Buccaneers), Reggie Moore (New York Jets), Jerel Myers (Buffalo Bills), Moran Morris (New Orleans Saints), Ed Newsome (Philadelphia Eagles) and Donald Jordan (Chicago Bears), among many others.

Although the father of three and grandfather of five is proud of the players who have turned pro, he is equally proud of players who did not step on the NFL's playing fields. After all, teaching the lessons of life has been Seals' most important game plan. "I try to teach all of my players that there's more to life than just playing football," says Seals, a former standout running back at Prairie View A&M University. "I try to teach them about values, character and making good decisions on and off the field. So it's not about how many games I've won over the years, or how many players I've sent to the NFL; it's about how many young men became better people because of what I helped instill in them."

BANKING ON SUCCESS

VANESSA T. REED

Community Reinvestment Act Manager,
Houston Market
Comerica Bank, Inc.

By Donald James

As the community reinvestment act manager for Comerica Bank, Inc., Vanessa T. Reed has an unwavering commitment to serve low-to-moderate income communities in the greater Houston area. This is a commitment that Reed takes to heart. Since 2007 she has been proactive in ensuring that Comerica Bank is an active participant in rendering services to create and support affordable housing projects, small business initiatives, financial literacy education and other endeavors that vastly empower various communities.

In addition, Reed ensures that Comerica is in compliance with the Community Reinvestment Act, which was passed by Congress in 1977 to make sure that banks serve all sectors of the community, inclusive of low-to-moderate neighborhoods. "I love what I do because it's close to my individual passions and interests in helping the community," says Reed. "Although this is something that I would do on my own, my position with Comerica allows me to do much more to empower communities." Reed first joined Comerica in 2000 as a senior credit specialist where she effectively coordinated work flow strategies, and creatively prepared loan packages for commercial real estate deals.

A native of New Orleans, Reed has always had a high aptitude for math. Throughout high school, she thought her career path would entail going to college, earning an undergraduate degree in accounting and eventually becoming a CPA. Reed, however, became interested in the banking industry while attending the University of New Orleans and working as a customer service representative at First National Bank of Commerce in the Crescent City. While working at First National, Reed saw a multiplicity of opportunities in the banking industry.

Additionally, she was encouraged by the accomplishments of Virgil Robinson, president and chief executive officer of Dryades Savings Bank and the accomplishments of other successful African Americans at Liberty Bank and Trust. Both black-owned banks are in New Orleans. "I didn't know him – Mr. Robinson – personally, but just the idea that this black man was the president of a bank intrigued me," explains Reed. "So he was definitely someone who I greatly admired and someone who inspired me to think about banking as a career."

After earning a bachelor's degree in business management, Reed continued to work for First National, followed by professional employment stints with Bellsouth Mobility and The Ellis Company, the latter of which is the largest African-American roofing company in the South. Upon moving to Houston in the late 1990s, Reed re-entered the banking industry with Comerica. Reed often thinks about Robinson's trailblazing banking career as she continues to blaze her own trails at Comerica. Since joining the bank 11 years ago, she has earned five Comerica ROAR awards for outstanding achievements. In addition, the community has recognized her contributions with such honors as, *rolling out* magazine's Top 25 Most Influential Women in Houston (2007), Houston Citizens Chamber of Commerce's first Spirit of the Community Award (2008) and the Texas Women's Empowerment Foundation's Volunteer Award (2010).

Although Reed's position at Comerica keeps her connected to the community, her personal civic and community involvements include serving on the boards of Change Happens! (formerly Families Under Urban and Social Attack), and the Houston Citizens Chamber of Commerce. She also volunteers quality time to the Texas Women's Empowerment Foundation. On a personal note, Reed has been married to Kevin J. Reed for 11 years. The couple is raising a young son and daughter.

PROPER PREPARATION AND PERFORMANCE

TERENCE H. FONTAINE

Group Vice President of Business Services
Metropolitan Transit Authority, Harris County

By Terreece M. Clarke

Terence Fontaine wants you to tell him that he can't do something. Tell him he can't, and he'll work day and night to surpass expectations. He describes himself as very competitive – an accurate description of someone who decided, as a child, to teach himself tennis so he could beat a competitive friend.

Fontaine's father worked for Delta Airlines for 32 years and encouraged him to become an airplane mechanic with job security.

"I understand that he was trying to protect me, but every time I saw a pilot walking down the concourse I'd say, 'That's me right there,'" explains Fontaine. "No one besides the Lord and me believed I could do it. The Marines claimed I was colorblind and a math teacher laughed at the thought of me becoming a pilot. I continued going to lessons, spending my own cash, getting flight hours in; I worked my butt off and not only became a pilot, I received an Airline Transport Pilot Certificate – the highest achievable level as an airline pilot."

While in the Marines he worked in aviation operations. After an honorable discharge Fontaine became a licensed aircraft technician and joined the Technical Operations division of Continental Airlines, becoming the airline's first African-American manager of Maintenance Operations. Fontaine transferred to the Flight Operations division where he worked as a pilot instructor on the Boeing 727. In 1998 he passed the Boeing 777 Captain's course logging several hundred domestic and international flight hours as an EMB-145 pilot.

In 2004 Mayor Bill White appointed Fontaine deputy chief of staff, but when Hurricane Katrina struck in 2005 he became the co-site manager for recovery efforts headquartered at George R. Brown Convention Center. The site received national recognition for impacting the lives of more than 28,000 evacuees and survivors. "That was a life-changing experience," Fontaine described. "All anyone wanted was to be treated with dignity and respect. It was a rewarding experience to be able to help."

In his current position as group vice president of business services for Houston's METRO, he has seven departments reporting to him with an annual budget of more than $60 million.

Fontaine is driven to go beyond success in the boardroom. Happily married with one daughter, he is earning a 4.0 GPA in his education doctorate program. He earned a Master of Business Administration degree from the University of Houston and a bachelor's degree in aviation from Southern Illinois University.

He is the chairman of the board for the Eldorado Social Club, a member of the Deacon's Board at Wheeler Avenue Baptist Church, the United Negro College Fund advisory board, the Houston Livestock Show Rodeo International and Corporate Development Committees, Alpha Phi Alpha Fraternity, Inc., the Houston Area Urban League, the Organization of Black Airline Pilots, the William A. Lawson Institute for Peace and Prosperity Advisory Board and Congressman Al Green's Military academy board.

"If you can't tell a story of how you've given back, if you can't recall names of people you've helped, then shame on you," says Fontaine. "I couldn't care less about folks' personal achievements. It's about who you've helped and who you've reached out to. It's not all about the money; it's about being a blessing to someone else's struggle."

Photo by Ken Jones

THE SPIRIT TO LEAD

D.Z. COFIELD

President
NAACP Houston Branch

By D.Z. Cofield

D.Z. Cofield is a native New Yorker, who has traveled across the world serving in the gospel of Jesus Christ. One of Cofield's many passions is his dedication to community service and beyond. He was often asked, "Why are you running for the presidency of the NAACP Houston Branch?" His response was simple-it's time. "I have watched the shifting landscape of our society and heard the frustration within our community. I want to be a part of the solution," he says. With an overwhelming response from the community, on November 18, 2010, Cofield was elected to serve as president of the NAACP Houston Branch. With this new challenge, his focus is to refocus the organization, redefine the fight and re-engage the membership and community in the cause.

In 1994 Cofield was chosen to serve as the senior pastor for the Good Hope Missionary Baptist Church in Houston, Texas. Good Hope has grown from a congregation of approximately 150 members to an active membership of more than 3,000. The church has had several extraordinary mission programs to be developed under the leadership and direction of Cofield.

He currently teaches nationally and internationally and is a former instructor at Dallas Theological Seminary and a former adjunct professor at the College of Biblical Studies-Houston. Cofield has received numerous honors and awards including the Presidential Scholarship Award at Dallas Theological Seminary, the H.A. Ironside Award for excellence in expository preaching, and was also listed in *Who's Who Among Students in Colleges and Universities* for three consecutive years. He has written for several Christian publications, including *Preaching Today, Leadership Journal* and the *African-American Pastors' Journal on Great Eulogies*.

Cofield serves as Hope Academy's superintendent. The academy, established in 2009, launched its inaugural year with 100 students and is a co-educational HISD Charter School that targets young people, grades 9-12, who are experiencing academic difficulty, behavioral challenges and other issues that have not allowed them to have success in a traditional school setting. Hope Academy serves young men and women who are considered to be at a high risk for academic failure as well as life skills failure, by addressing many of the issues and obstacles they face which put them at a tremendous disadvantage in the pursuit of a normal, healthy adult life.

After graduating from Swarthmore College in Swarthmore, Pennsylvania, he earned a master's degree in theology at the Dallas Theological Seminary and a Doctor of Ministry degree at Faith Evangelical Seminary in Tacoma, Washington.

Cofield is the proud father of three: two boys, Marques and Brandon, and one girl, Tiffany. He is a certified scuba diver for more than 12 years now, is an avid reader and enjoys music and traveling.

D.Z. COFIELD

The Bulsard Group, LLC
Your Partner in Creating a New Tomorrow

Lean Six Sigma • Change Management • Operational Excellence

Using our *12-Point Approach* and *7-6-5 Process,*
we will partner with you to:

1. *ASSESS* your current state organizational capability.

2. *DEVELOP* a customized strategy to transformational success using one or more of our 12-Points.

3. *GUIDE* and mentor your organization through your strategy in our proven 7-stage plan.

The Value Experts

The Bulsard Group, LLC • 1415 S. Voss, Suite 110-459 • Houston, TX 77057
Web: www.bulsardgroup.com • Email: info@bulsardgroup.com • Phone: (832) 428-1484

PRAIRIE VIEW A&M UNIVERSITY
NORTHWEST HOUSTON CENTER

Closer than you think.

Apply today!
www.pvamu.edu/northwest

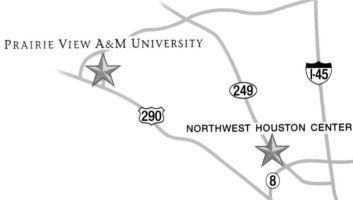

PRAIRIE VIEW A&M UNIVERSITY

I-45

249

290

NORTHWEST HOUSTON CENTER

8

Houston

610

I-10

RUN A MARATHON

SON'S MEDICAL SCHOOL

TRIP TO PARIS

TIME WITH GRANDSON

REMODEL KITCHEN

VOLUNTEER

With you when *you need a Financial Advisor fully invested in you*

You have many options if you are looking to create a retirement plan based on your current situation. But creating a plan that will help get you to your dreams requires a more personal approach. At Wells Fargo Advisors, we'll look at your entire financial picture, even money you've invested elsewhere, before creating a strategy that will help get you to and through retirement. With more than 125 years of investment experience, Wells Fargo Advisors offers more than just knowledge and insight. We offer vision and a path to lead you. To learn more about our comprehensive approach, call today.

Together we'll go far

INVESTMENTS · PLANNING · RETIREMENT

Ollie B. Harris, III
Vice President - Investments
2700 Post Oak Blvd., Ste 800
Houston, TX 77056
713-629-2103
OLLIE.HARRIS@wfadvisors.com

Investment and Insurance Products: ▶ **NOT FDIC Insured** ▶ **NO Bank Guarantee** ▶ **MAY Lose Value**

Wheeler Avenue Baptist Church

WHERE WE WORSHIP JESUS CHRIST
AND MINISTER TO THE TOTAL PERSON

Worship Services
Sundays at 7:15am, 9:00am, 11:00am and 1:00pm
Sunday School
9:00am
Wednesday Bible Study
12noon and 7:00pm

Location
3826 Wheeler Avenue
Houston, Texas 77004
713-748-5240
www.wheeleravebc.org

Rev. Dr. Marcus D. Cosby, Senior Pastor
Rev. William A. Lawson, Pastor Emeritus

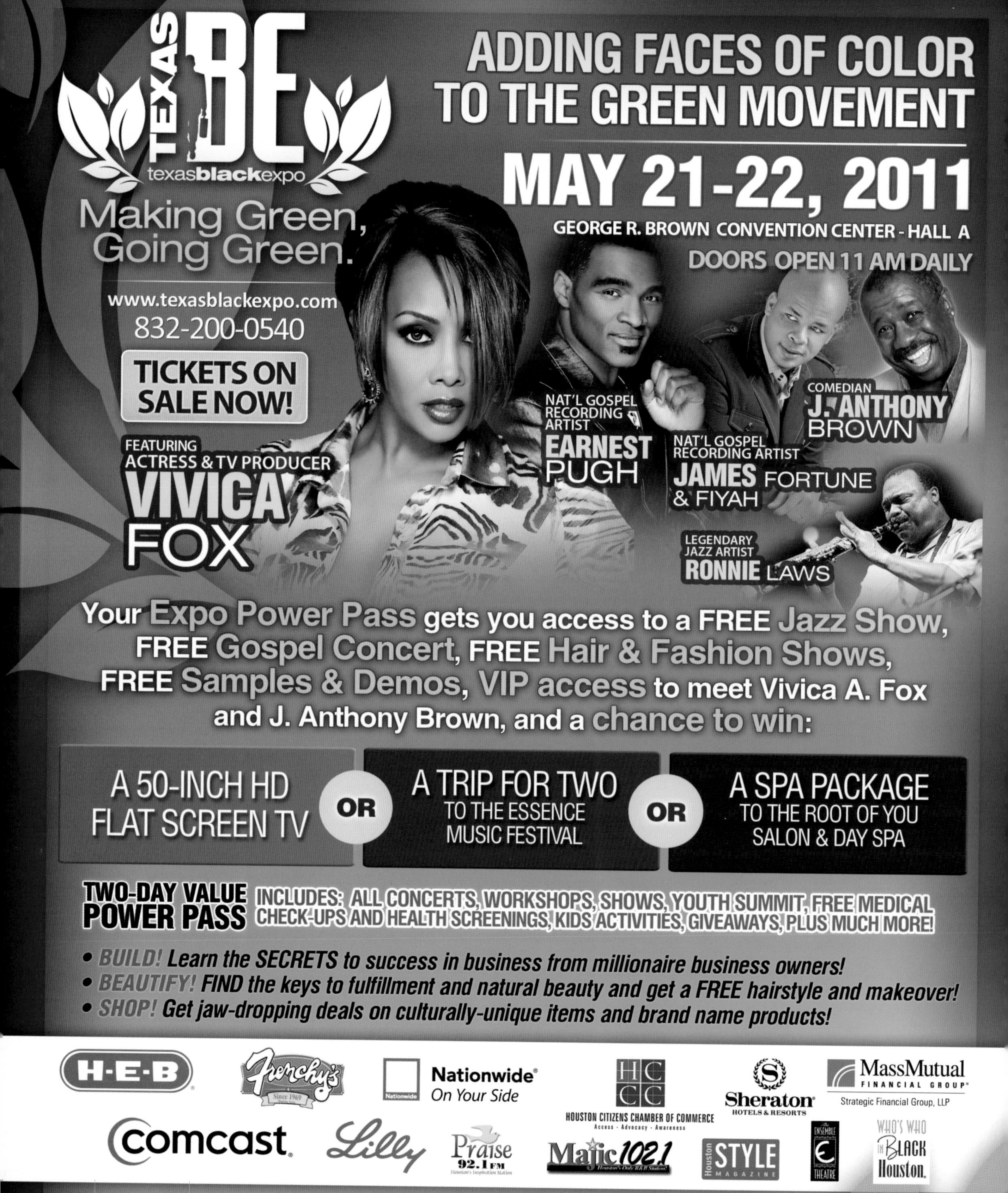

TEXAS BE
texasblackexpo

Making Green, Going Green.

www.texasblackexpo.com
832-200-0540

TICKETS ON SALE NOW!

FEATURING
ACTRESS & TV PRODUCER
VIVICA FOX

ADDING FACES OF COLOR TO THE GREEN MOVEMENT

MAY 21-22, 2011

GEORGE R. BROWN CONVENTION CENTER - HALL A
DOORS OPEN 11 AM DAILY

NAT'L GOSPEL RECORDING ARTIST
EARNEST PUGH

NAT'L GOSPEL RECORDING ARTIST
JAMES FORTUNE & FIYAH

COMEDIAN
J. ANTHONY BROWN

LEGENDARY JAZZ ARTIST
RONNIE LAWS

Your Expo Power Pass gets you access to a FREE Jazz Show, FREE Gospel Concert, FREE Hair & Fashion Shows, FREE Samples & Demos, VIP access to meet Vivica A. Fox and J. Anthony Brown, and a chance to win:

A 50-INCH HD FLAT SCREEN TV   OR   **A TRIP FOR TWO** TO THE ESSENCE MUSIC FESTIVAL   OR   **A SPA PACKAGE** TO THE ROOT OF YOU SALON & DAY SPA

TWO-DAY VALUE POWER PASS INCLUDES: ALL CONCERTS, WORKSHOPS, SHOWS, YOUTH SUMMIT, FREE MEDICAL CHECK-UPS AND HEALTH SCREENINGS, KIDS ACTIVITIES, GIVEAWAYS, PLUS MUCH MORE!

- *BUILD!* Learn the SECRETS to success in business from millionaire business owners!
- *BEAUTIFY!* FIND the keys to fulfillment and natural beauty and get a FREE hairstyle and makeover!
- *SHOP!* Get jaw-dropping deals on culturally-unique items and brand name products!

BRANWARWINE
DISTRIBUTING CO.

Branwar South African Wines

Founder Wayne Luckett & son Warren

Branwar Wine Distributing Co.
Importer and Distributor of South African Wines

Branwar, derived from son's name Brandon and Warren, serves as an importing and wholesale distribution company for South African wines across the United States. Branwar's current focus is on the Texas wine market. Their wines are now available in Houston, San Antonio and Austin.

For Branwar's portfolio of South African wines and a location near you, please visit www.branwarwines.com .

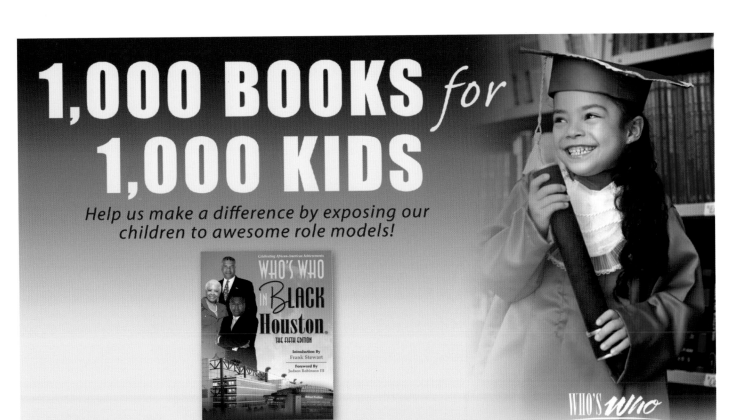
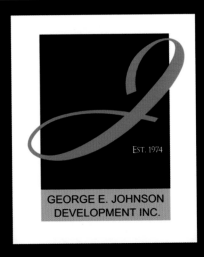

GEORGE E. JOHNSON DEVELOPMENT INC.

Established in 1974 as Johnson and Sons Realty the company has evolved into ...

GEORGE E. JOHNSON DEVELOPMENT INC.

One of the most comprehensive Real Estate Development companies in the country. George E. Johnson Development specializes in Commercial and Residential Real Estate Services, Construction, Interior Design and Community Development.

"Large enough to serve you....Small enough to care"

Commercial Real Estate

Residential Real Estate

Construction

Interior Design

Community Development

"Developing Visions"

George E. Johnson Development Inc.
12401 S. Post Oak Road,
Suite 100
Houston, Texas 77045

713-721-5555

www.GeorgeJohnsonDev.com

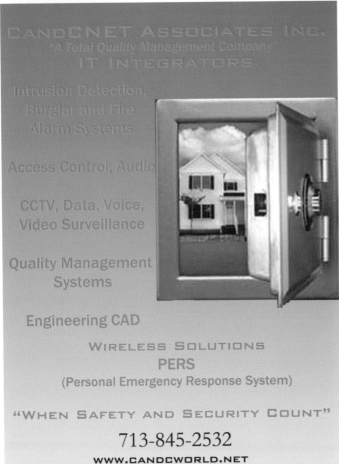

BE HEARD
your world, your voice, our work

INTEGRATED MARKETING   MULTI-MEDIA   EXTENDED NETWORK

Let Real Times Media create unique and innovative marketing experiences for your brand.

REAL TIMES MEDIA

Real Times Media 535 Grisworld, Suite 1300, Detroit, MI 48226 ▪ 313-963-8100

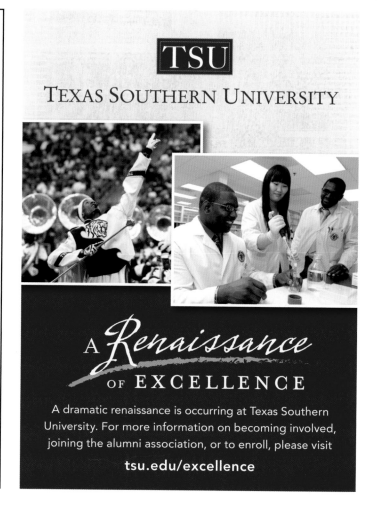

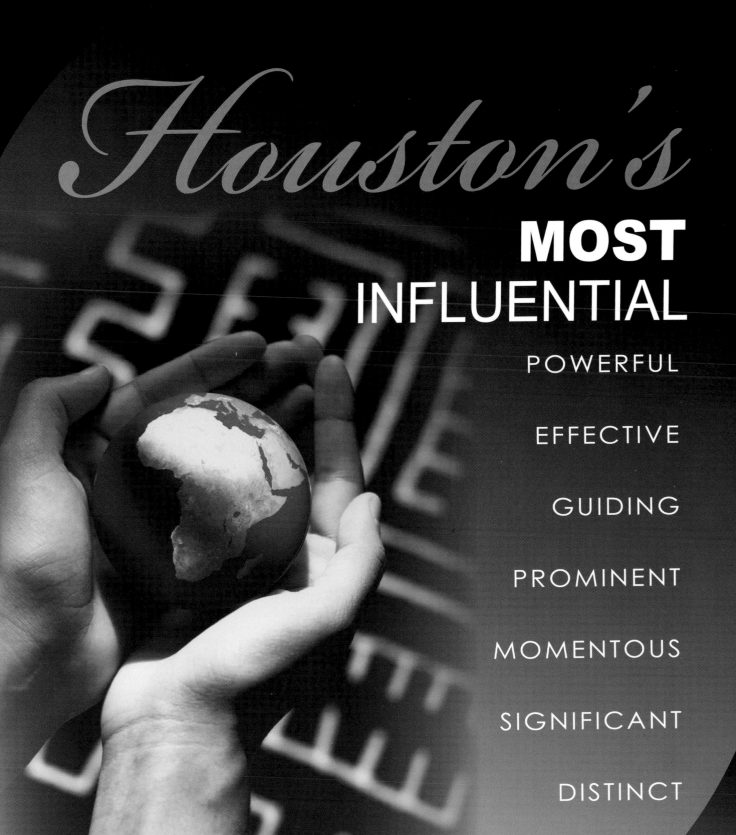

Houston's
MOST
INFLUENTIAL

POWERFUL

EFFECTIVE

GUIDING

PROMINENT

MOMENTOUS

SIGNIFICANT

DISTINCT

LEADING

MEANINGFUL

The Honorable Dr. Alma A. Allen

State Representative District 131
Texas House of Representatives

Errol Allen II

Program Integrator
NASA

Prior to being elected to the Texas House of Representatives, Dr. Alma A. Allen served as an elected member of the State Board of Education for more than 10 years, and an educator in the Houston Independent School District for 39 years. Currently, Allen serves on the Committee on Corrections as vice chair, Committee on Public Education and the Committee on House Administration.

Allen's honors include the Houston Area Alliance of Black School Educators' Living Legend Award, for dedication and activism in education, Principal of the Year, District V, Outstanding Alumnus of the University of Houston and Texas Freedom Network's Walking the Walk Award.

Allen and husband, Lawrence Allen, Sr.(deceased), are the parents of Dr. Patricia Allen, principal of MacGregor Elementary School, and Lawrence Allen Jr., HISD Senior community relations liaison and elected member of the State Board of Education, and grandparents of five grandchildren, and one great-grandchild.

Errol Allen II is a program integrator in the Office of the Chief Financial Officer for NASA at the Johnson Space Center. At NASA, Allen manages the center budgets for seven space programs, which account for approximately $200 million in federal appropriations.

Allen co-chairs the Student Affairs Committee for the Houston Chapter of the National Black MBA Association Inc., which facilitates the Leaders of Tomorrow high school mentoring program. He also serves as director of educational activities for the Alpha Eta Lambda Chapter of Alpha Phi Alpha Fraternity, Inc. Allen sits on the board of directors for the Foundation for Student Leadership and Success. In addition, he volunteers on the finance team for the Houston Citizens Chamber of Commerce and is an active member of the Houston Area Urban League Young Professionals.

A native of Houston, Texas, and a graduate of Florida A&M University, Allen earned a Bachelor of Science degree in management and a Master of Business Administration degree, with a concentration in finance.

The Honorable
Willie E.B. Blackmon

Retired Judge
Municipal Court
City of Houston

Stephen K. Brown II

Chairman
Fort Bend County Democratic Party

The Honorable Willie E.B. Blackmon is a licensed attorney in Michigan, Nebraska and Texas. He retired from his position as municipal judge with the City of Houston in 2004.

A highly decorated officer, Blackmon entered the U.S. Air Force as a judge advocate in 1984. During a distinguished career which spanned 28 years, he served with the active duty force, the reserves, the National Guard and earned the rank of lieutenant colonel. Prior to his military retirement, he was named as a co-recipient of the Gerald Ford Medal for Distinguished Public Service.

In 2005 he received the Texas A&M University Distinguished Alumnus Award, and was inducted into the Texas Black Sports Hall of Fame in 2009. He is slated for induction into the Prairie View Interscholastic League Coaches Association Hall of Fame in the summer of 2011.

A native Houstonian, Blackmon is a lifetime member of Alpha Phi Alpha Fraternity, Inc. He received a bachelor's degree in marketing from Texas A&M University and a juris doctorate degree from Texas Southern University, Thurgood Marshall School of Law.

Stephen Brown joined the staff of U.S. Congresswoman Sheila Jackson Lee before accepting a position as budget analyst for House Appropriations Subcommittee Chairman Sylvester Turner in Austin, Texas. Soon after the 76th Legislative Session, he accepted a fellowship to attend graduate school at the University of New Orleans where he studied urban and minority politics.

As a result of that success, Stephen later launched Capitol Assets, A Full Service Public Affairs firm. In that role he was involved in a statewide public education and lobbying efforts on behalf of the American Heart Association to secure support for pending childhood obesity and anti-smoking legislation. He also represented Houston METRO at the State Capitol and served as the public affairs strategist to the Chief executive officers of the Houston, Dallas and Austin branches of the National Urban League.

In March 2010, Stephen was elected the Chairman of the Fort Bend County Democratic Party.

Stephen serves on the Missouri City Tax Increment Reinvestment Zone #3, and is a member of the Xi Kappa Lambda chapter of Alpha Phi Alpha, Fraternity Inc.

He is the husband of Monique Mathis Brown and proud father of Stephen III and Mathis.

The Honorable Jacqueline (Jacquie) Baly Chaumette

Councilmember, City of Sugar Land
President, BalyProjects, LLC
Adjunct Professor University of Houston

The Honorable Rodney Ellis

Senator, District 13
Texas Senate

In May 2008, Jacqueline (Jacquie) Baly Chaumette won election to Sugar Land's City Council with more than 69 percent of the vote. She became the only black person, only woman and youngest member on council. Jacquie was unopposed in her re-election bid in 2010. Chaumette is president and chief executive officer of BalyProjects and a political science professor at the University of Houston. She has been featured on several radio stations discussing policy matters.

Jacquie serves on several boards including: Texas Lyceum, Greater Houston Partnership's Transportation Infrastructure Committee, Houston-Galveston Area Council's Transportation Policy Council, Sugar Land's Economic Development Board, Texas CASA, YMCA (past president), Alley Theatre Advisory Board, Houston Community College Advisory Committee, Houston City Hall Fellows, Commonwealth Elementary and Fort Settlement Middle School PTAs, Fort Bend Boys' Choir as president and the Women's Resource of Greater Houston.

A native of St. Croix, U.S. Virgin Islands, Jacquie holds a bachelor's degree in political science and a master's degree in city planning with an emphasis in public policy. She is a classically trained flutist. She and her husband David have two sons, Raphael, 13, and Alexandre, 10.

Senator Rodney Ellis was first elected to represent District 13 in the Texas Senate in 1990. During his tenure, he has earned praise as a leader on economic development, education, civil rights, responsible environmental policy, tax cuts for the middle class, criminal justice, and workforce development issues.

Ellis is the current chairman of the Senate Committee on Government Organization, which looks at measures to improve the efficiency of state government. He also sits on the Senate State Affairs, Criminal Justice, and Transportation and Homeland Security Committees.

Ellis currently serves on the National Commission on Energy Policy, the University of Texas School of Law Foundation Board, the Council on Foreign Relations, the Rainbow PUSH Coalition Board of Directors, the Alliance for Digital Equality Board of Advisors, chairs the Board of Directors for the Innocence Project, Inc. of New York, and co-chairs the Commission to Engage African Americans on Climate Change.

He is married to Licia Green-Ellis and has four children.

Dr. Reagan Flowers

Founder & Chief Executive Officer
CSTEM

Larry V. Green

Chief Executive Officer
HoustonWorks USA

In 2002, Dr. Reagan Flowers coined the term "STEM" when she developed C-STEM to support teacher development, real-world problem-solving, and application of learning within Pre-K-12 classrooms. Having grown CSTEM from a single middle school campus to an international Pre K-12 program with outreach impacting more than 50,000 students and now operating in more than 50 schools in six states and the Dominican Republic, Flowers has demonstrated through action, an expertise in partnership development, educational leadership, and an entrepreneurial spirit.

Flowers authored two books, *The CSTEM Challenge: A Feeder Pattern Approach to Reaching All Students through Hands-on Project-based Learning* and *CSTEM Pedagogy: Your Guide to Project-Based Learning*. She currently serves on numerous board of the STEM Education Coalition, she is chair for the STEM Education sub-committee for the Texas Business and Education Coalition and vice chair of the American Leadership Forum Houston Chapter.

Flowers received a bachelor's degree in biology from Texas Southern University, a master's degree in counseling from Prairie View A&M University of Texas, and Doctor of Philosophy degree in Educational Leadership from the Union Institute & University.

Larry V. Green, chief executive officer of HoustonWorks USA, has more than 20 years of progressively responsible experience directing more than 500 employees in organizations with revenues in excess of $23 million.

Green lead the Washington, D.C., office of the Thurgood Marshall College Fund, serving as vice president of development and government affairs and district director to United States Congresswoman Sheila Jackson Lee. As principle Partner in his law firm, Larry V. Green & Associates, He focused on employment, corporate, labor and business law.

Green is a member of the Greater Houston Partnership, a board member of the National Workforce Association, a member and former board Trustee of Brentwood Baptist Church, a member of Alpha Phi Alpha Fraternity, Inc., serves on the College of Science and Technology advisory board at Texas Southern University and was elected to serve on the Board of the Greater Houston Convention and Visitors Bureau. He is also an alumnus of the Center for Houston's Future.

Green holds Bachelor of Arts deree in political science from the University of Houston and a doctorate of jurisprudence degree, from the Thurgood Marshall School of Law, Texas Southern University.

James E. Harris

Director
Supplier Diversity
H-E-B

Mayerland Harris

Group Vice President
Human Resources
H-E-B

As director of diversity and supplier diversity for H-E-B, James Harris is responsible for developing and implementing diversity management strategic initiatives. He is also responsible for driving the company supplier diversity programs by ensuring the company's procurement entities create an environment of inclusion for small and minority business enterprises. These processes increase the company's level of engagement with partners (employees), customers and communities they serve.

James serves on the boards of the World Youth Foundation, Houston Minority Council's SDAC (Supplier Diversity Advisory Council), Texas Diversity Council, Texas NAACP Corporate Advisory Council, Texas Business Alliance Advisory Board, American Heart Association's Health Equity, is vice chair of the Southwest Minority Supplier Development Council and H-E-B's Health & Wellness Corporate Council.

James obtained a bachelor's degree in political science from Alcorn State University. He has been married to his wife, Shavonda, for 26 years and has two children, Carmen and Brandon.

Mayerland Harris, group vice president of human resources for H-E-B, is a dynamic and influential leader and team builder with more than 26 years of retail experience in human resources and store operations. She leads a team of more than 50 HR professionals including field managers, recruiters, training and development managers and a full administrative staff. She is directly responsible for providing leadership to all Human Resources functions for nearly 75 H-E-B stores, the Central Market Division, as well as the manufacturing, warehousing and transportation divisions.

Her leadership team is accountable for the implementation of policies and programs including employment, employee relations, benefits, compensation, training and employee assistance.

Mayerland received a bachelor's degree from the University of Texas at Austin in 1991 and a Master of Business Administration degree from Texas A&M University in 2007. She received her certification of senior professional in human resources in 1999.

Originally from Austin, she is married and has two wonderful children.

Harry J. Hayes

Director
Solid Waste Management
City of Houston

Winell Herron

Group Vice President,
Public Affairs, Diversity & Environmental Affairs
H-E-B

Harry J. Hayes is Houston's Solid Waste Management Department (SWMD) director where he oversees a $67 million budget for solid waste services, recycling, transfer stations, and the city's debris management operations.

Hayes led the SWMD and contractor forces through record-breaking efforts after Hurricane Ike with more than 75 percent of the debris collected in the first 30 days. This was the largest Texas recycling project where 100 percent of all vegetative debris was recycled.

A fiscal hawk, Hayes cut his budget by millions. He renegotiated the contract for disposal and transfer stations which reduced the city's disposal payments by more than $8 million annually and up to $200 million over the previous terms. The Yard Waste program resulted in 100 percent diversion and $1.5 million savings.

A Texas Southern University graduate and a 1985 Connaissance de la France graduate of the Universite de Bordeaux, Hayes also served as an enlisted member and an officer in the U.S. Army Reserves.

Hayes is married with three children.

A dynamic leader with strong ties in the community, Winell, leads H-E-B's public affairs, diversity and environmental affairs initiatives across the state.

Winell began her career at H-E-B in 1988 in store operations. She was later promoted to service team leader then to director of workforce diversity. In February of 1999, she was promoted to vice president of customer service, and later to group vice president of diversity and people development. In April of 2002, she was appointed to her current position.

Winell earned a bachelor's degree in business administration from the University of Texas at Austin. She completed the Food Industry Management Program at the University of Southern California and received a Master of Business Administration degree from the University of Texas at San Antonio.

Winell is highly involved in the community and serves on the board of Texans Care for Children, The Ensemble Theatre, Girl Scouts, Big Brothers Big Sisters and serves on the board of trustees for the University of Incarnate Word. She also chairs the Texas NAACP Corporate Advisory Council.

She and her husband, William, reside in Houston.

The Honorable Jolanda "Jo" Jones

Councilmember at Large
Houston City Council

The Honorable Sheila Jackson Lee

Representative, 18th District of Texas
U.S. House of Representatives

Jolanda "Jo" Jones, an attorney by profession, represents all Houstonians as an atlarge councilmember, successfully fights to reform the criminal justice system, diligently contributes to charitable organizations and does all she can do to support her honors graduate son, Jiovanni, a freshman in college.

Because Jones' family lived in historically disadvantaged neighborhoods, affordable housing and the criminal justice system are her passions. Jones is used to being David in struggles against modern-day Goliaths. She was instrumental in bringing to light the serious problems at the Houston Police Department Crime Lab, refusing to back down because innocent people were being convicted and criminals were going free. She took on a powerful state legislator when he took the small child of a poor immigrant and won—reuniting a family that would have been forever broken without her help. As chair of the Housing and Community Development Committee, Jones is tireless in her effort to weed out and reverse incompetence in the City Housing Department.

Jones will never forget where she came from which is why she will always fight to ensure all are treated fairly.

Congresswoman Sheila Jackson Lee is serving her seventh term as a member of the U.S. House of Representatives. She represents the 18th Congressional District of Texas, centered in Houston. Jackson Lee earned a Bachelor of Arts degree in political science from Yale University, with honors, followed by a juris doctorate degree from the University of Virginia Law School. In the 110th Congress, Jackson Lee was named the new chairwoman of the Homeland Security Subcommittee on Transportation Security and Infrastructure Protection.

She sits on three congressional committees: the House committees on the Judiciary, Homeland Security and Foreign Affairs. Jackson Lee is a founder, member and co-chair of the Congressional Children's Caucus, the Pakistan Caucus, the Afghan Caucus and the Algerian Caucus.

Jackson Lee has been hailed by *Ebony* magazine as one of the 100 Most Fascinating Black Women of the 20th century. *Congressional Quarterly* named her one of the 50 most effective members of Congress. *U.S. News & World Report* named her one of the 10 most influential legislators in the House of Representatives.

Eric Lyons

President & Chief Executive Officer
Houston Citizens Chamber of Commerce

Carl McGowan

Regional Marketing Director
Texas & Oklahoma United Healthcare

Eric Lyons is the President and chief executive officer of the Houston Citizens Chamber of Commerce. He is an experienced entrepreneur and an accomplished business professional. He has successfully led the Houston Citizens Chamber of Commerce, which is the largest African-American chamber of commerce in Houston and second oldest in the nation, in growing its membership base and executing collaborative engagements with corporate and community stakeholders.

He received his bachelor's degree in Chemical Engineering and a Master of Business Administration degree in marketing and management from the University of Tennessee. As an entrepreneur, he has served as a principal with Impact Strategies Consultants, a boutique consulting firm. Also, he has 17 years of experience in sales, marketing and account management in multiple industries with a proven record of achieving results.

He has served on the boards of the Texas A&M MBA program, Breakthrough Houston, Alpha Phi Alpha Fraternity, Inc. and other community organizations.

Carl McGowan is the regional marketing director for Texas and Oklahoma at United Healthcare. The native of Detroit earned his undergraduate degree from Dartmouth College, where he majored in economics and government, and Master of Business Administration degree from the Ross School of Business at the University of Michigan, where he was a consortium fellow.

Outside of work, Carl serves as president of the National Black MBA Association, Houston Chapter, and as chairman of Act One, an auxiliary of The Ensemble Theatre. He has received several awards for his professional and community work, including the Distinguished Alumni Award from the Consortium for Graduate Study in Management President's Circle member with the Houston Area Urban League, and 2010 40 Under 40 recognition from the Houston Business Journal.

In addition to his nonprofit leadership roles, Carl is a member of several other organizations including the Dartmouth College and University of Michigan Alumni Associations, the National Urban League, and the American Marketing Association. He is a life member of Alpha Phi Alpha Fraternity, Inc., and the National Black MBA Association.

Carl resides in Houston, Texas, where he attends Windsor Village United Methodist Church.

Eugene "Gene" Padgett

Director, U.S. Operations Accounting
Spectra Energy Corp

Laurence Payne

Past Chairman
Board of the Education
Harris County

Eugene "Gene" Padgett is president of the Houston Chapter for the National Association of Black Accountants, Inc. Gene, a native of Rochester, New York, is a graduate of Prairie View A&M University.

After six years with PricewaterhouseCoopers LLP, Gene joined Duke Energy in 1999, and was responsible for the research of several accounting issues on a reactive basis, as well as on a proactive basis, by monitoring and implementing standard setter changes. In August of 2002, Gene relocated to Houston and transferred with Duke to assume the role of controller for Duke's Canadian division, Westcoast Energy Inc.

In 2007, the gas transmission segment of Duke was spun-off and made public as Spectra Energy. As a result, Gene assumed the role as general manager of corporate accounting and research for Spectra.

In January of 2011, Gene assumed the role of director of U.S. operations accounting. In this capacity, Gene is responsible for the day-to-day management of the flow of natural gas, revenue billing and capital spending in excess of $1 billion annually.

Gene has held board positions with several organizations and associations.

Laurence Payne has 34 years of experience in public service, education and not-for-profit leadership. Larry is recognized from City Hall to the White House with city, state and national leaders actively seek out his counsel.

Larry recently served as president and chief executive officer of Houston Habitat for Humanity. During his tenure he increased home production threefold and personally secured an endowment from Oprah Winfrey for 65 houses. Leaving Habitat for Humanity, Larry currently serves as the past chairman of the Board of the Education Foundation of Harris County serving the children of its 26 school districts.

Larry's career in public service includes notable positions at the city, state and congressional levels. Larry helped bring the 1991 and 2002 National NAACP Conventions to Houston where he served as general chairman.

Larry brought his interest to the public with a weekly TV show *Dialogue Houston* where he deals with issues of diversity and race relations in the Greater Houston area. Larry's show airs on Houston Community College (HCC-TV). Larry added *Interchange*, a weekly radio show on KPFT-FM (90.1).

Larry has actively participated in the several community organizations.

Dr. Jonita W. Reynolds

Chief Executive Officer
Gulf Coast Community Services Association Inc.

The Honorable Ronald Reynolds

State Representative
District 27, Fort Bend County

Dr. Jonita Reynolds is the chief executive officer of Gulf Coast Community Services Association, Inc. an organization dedicated to strengthening the educational, social and economic well-being of the unserved and underserved in Harris County. With an annual budget of $25 million and 350 FTEs, they provide high-quality educational, financial and workforce development services in an effort to transition those most in need into a more economically independent state.

This former Ms. Black World-Houston received the following honors: American Red Cross' Humanitarian Award; *Style Magazine*'s Top 5 Most Stylish Citizens; *rolling out* magazine's 25 Most Influential Women; D-MARS Women In It to Win It and YMCA Minority Achiever. She is active with the Bay Ridge Christian College Board of Trustees, NAACP, American Leadership Forum, Missouri City Links, Top Ladies, and Alpha Kappa Alpha Sorority, Inc.

Reynolds is a magna cum laude graduate from the University of Houston where she also earned master's and doctorate degrees in education.

A native of Houston, Reynolds is happily married to State Representative Ronald Reynolds. Her mantra is to be "deeply rooted, ever-growing, and forever serving."

Ron Reynolds is state representative for Fort Bend County's House District 27. Ron is managing partner in the law firm of Brown, Brown & Reynolds, P.C.

Ron serves as president of the Missouri City & Vicinity Branch NAACP, FBISD Bond Advisory Committee and is past president of the Houston Lawyers Association.

Ron has the distinction of being one of the youngest people appointed to serve as an associate municipal judge for The City of Houston. He was also an adjunct professor at Texas Southern University. He also serves as vice president of the Fort Bend Democrats, Fort Bend ISD Bond Advisory Committee and Constable Ruben Davis Advisory Council. Ron is past president of the Houston Lawyers Association.

Ron has received numerous achievement awards for his legal and civic engagement. Recently, he was voted Best Attorney in Houston by *H Texas* Magazine.

He attended Texas Southern University and received a bachelor's degree in public affairs, magna cum laude. Ron received a doctor of jurisprudence degree from Texas Tech University School of Law.

Ron is most proud and grateful for his wife, Dr. Jonita Reynolds, and his daughter, Lacey Reynolds.

Carroll G. Robinson

Associate Professor
Barbara Jordan-Mickey Leland
School of Public Affairs

Judson W. Robinson III

President & Chief Executive Officer
Houston Area Urban League

Carroll G. Robinson is an associate professor at Texas Southern University's (TSU) Barbara Jordan-Mickey Leland School of Public Affairs where he teaches in the Master of Public Administration program. He is co-principal investigator of the TSU National Transportation Security Center of Excellence-Petrochemical.

Carroll is a former at-large member of the Houston City Council where he served as chairman of the Transportation, Technology and Infrastructure Committee. He is chairman of the Houston Citizens Chamber of Commerce, the oldest and largest African-American chamber in Houston. Carroll is also third vice president of the NAACP, Houston Branch. He is a life member of the NAACP and Omega Psi Phi Fraternity, Inc.

Carroll received a Bachelor of Arts degree from Richard Stockton State College in Pomona, New Jersey and his law degree from George Washington University in Washington, D.C.

Judson W. Robinson III is a native Houstonian with more than 30 years of political and business experience. He began his professional career at IBM. After completing a successful career in IT, he went into politics and was elected to Houston City Council. He served as vice mayor pro tem from 1994 to 1996, then chaired four council committees and served on six others including the Committee on Business and Tourism, which he founded. He also chaired the Redevelopment and Revitalization Committee and under his leadership, the Hilton America's Convention Center Hotel project was begun, Midtown Redevelopment was launched and the city's first Downtown Grand Prix Auto Race was initiated.

In January of 2008, Judson became the new president and chief executive officer of the Houston Area Urban League. He continues involvement with nonprofit organizations including the Houston Wellness Association, Mental Health America of Houston, the Uptown Redevelopment Authority and is a proud supporter of the United Way of Greater Houston.

Judson received a bachelor's degree from Fisk University. He is married to Cora Robinson and the proud father of three children and one grandchild.

Dr. Gary J. Sheppard

Internal Medicine Physician
Southwest Memorial Physicians

Karen Y. Williams

Assistant Director For Public Services
City of Houston Municipal Courts

Gary J. Sheppard is a private practice Internist at Southwest Houston. He has been in practice for 16 years and although he is a general internist, he concentrates on hypertension and diabetes mellitus.

Gary is the current chairman of the board of trustees of the National Medical Association. He is the immediate past chief of staff of Memorial Hermann Southwest and was the first African American to hold the office. He is an active member of Houston Medical Forum, Harris County Medical Society, Texas Medical Association, Lone Star State Medical Society, National Medical Association and American Medical Association.

Gary received a Bachelor of Arts degree from Baylor University and a medical degree from The University of Texas Medical Branch at Galveston. He completed his residency at The University of Texas Health Science Center at Houston.

Gary is very active at his church, Wheeler Ave. Baptist, where he serves as a trustee, a member of the Courtesy Corps, an elder in the Boys Rights of Passage program and co-director of the WABC Bells of Praise Choir.

Karen Y. Williams is an assistant director for the City of Houston Municipal Courts Department. In this position, she oversees the call center, mail operations and the collection of more than $50 million in state and local revenue. Known for innovation, she infuses technology and best practices into the daily operations of the department for an enhanced customer experience and improved revenue collection.

Karen is also an entrepreneur; she is the co-founder and senior vice president of The Karsan Corporation, LLC, which operates businesses in leadership consulting, retail pharmacies and real estate investments. She is an active member of Houston's Gamma Phi Sigma Chapter of Sigma Gamma Rho Sorority, Inc., and holds a seat on its international board of directors, winning its highest award in 2008. Karen is also an active member of New Light Church.

Karen earned a bachelor's degree in political science and communications from the University of Wisconsin-Madison and a master's degree from Clark Atlanta University.

A native of Milwaukee, Wisconsin, Karen is the wife of Dr. Santana M. Williams and the proud mother of Karsan and Kendall.

Mark A. Williams

President, Chief Executive Officer &
Managing Partner
Protectors Insurance & Financial Services LLC

Michael Terry Williams

Regional Vice President of Operations
H-E-B

Mark A. Williams is the president, chief executive officer and managing partner of Protectors Insurance and Financial Services, LLC, a firm with more than 40 years of experience assisting clients with their insurance and financial services needs. Mark oversees the daily operations and assists in the business development area of the firm.

Mark is a graduate of the University of Texas at Austin with a Bachelor of Science degree in economics. His expertise comes from having more than 19 years of experience in the insurance and financial services arena. He holds several professional licenses throughout the United States, including general lines agent – Property and Casualty Insurance, general lines agent – Life, Accident, Health, and HMO Insurance, and Series 6 & 63 – FINRA Registered Representative licenses.

Mark currently serves as the chairman of the 100 Black Men of Metropolitan Houston, board Member for Dominion Community Development Corporation, past board member for the Houston Citizens Chamber of Commerce, national board member of the 100 Black Men of America, Inc., and member of Kappa Alpha Psi Fraternity, Inc.

Mark is the proud father of (two) children, Marcus and Haley.

Michael Terry Williams is a regional vice president of operations for H-E-B grocery stores. He has more than 30 years of grocery experience and is highly regarded as an expert in his field and is a respected influential leader and mentor.

Williams is a board member with the SHSU Alumni Association, the UNCF, End Hunger, Good Gang and H-E-B Credit Union. He is a campaign chairman for the United Way.

Williams is the recipient of the Houston Diversity Leadership Award, and the David Ashworth Humanitiy Award.

Williams graduated from Sam Houston State University, and completed the executive studies program at Cornell University. He also attended the University of Houston, and is a member of Omega Psi Phi Fraternity, Inc.

Williams is married to Joycelyn, and they have four beautiful children.

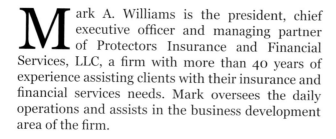

Houston's
CORPORATE BRASS

PROFICIENT

EXCEL

OUTSHINE

SURPASS

TRANSCEND

ENHANCE

SURMOUNT

MASTER

TRIUMPH

Alaina King Benford

Partner, Attorney at Law
Fulbright & Jaworski LLP

Alaina Benford is a litigation partner with Fulbright & Jaworski LLP. With a decade of experience trying cases in state and federal courts, she represents Fortune 500 corporations and individual clients in energy and real estate litigation, including eminent domain and condemnation matters and defends some of the world's largest energy companies against catastrophic personal injury claims.

In 2006 Alaina was named a Texas Rising Star in civil litigation in *Law & Politics* magazine and in 2008 she was one of Houston's top lawyers in business litigation in *H Texas* magazine. This year, she is a recipient of the 2011 Audrey H. Lawson IMPACT Award.

Alaina received a bachelor's degree from Texas Southern University and graduated, magna cum laude, from Thurgood Marshall School of Law. She serves on the executive board of directors of The Ensemble Theatre and the board of trustees at Annunciation Orthodox School. As a member of Wheeler Avenue Baptist Church, she helped establish the church's legal ministry and Will-a-thon.

Alaina is married to Leo Benford and they have two sons, Leo Wesley and Langston.

Pamela Ellis Benson

National Account Executive
Greater Houston Convention and
Visitors Bureau

Pamela is a national account executive for the Greater Houston Convention and Visitors Bureau (GHCVB). In this position she attracts and secures conventions and meetings of various sizes for the city of Houston from corporate, association, religious and ethnic markets.

Pamela has been a leader and trendsetter in the hospitality industry for over 25 years. Along with her support team at the GHCVB, she recently spear- headed the efforts in securing one of the largest conferences in the religious market. ELCA will yield an overall economic impact for the city of Houston of over 35 million.

In addition, Pamela is currently a chartered member of the Pearland Chapter of Top Ladies of Distinction, Inc. She accepted the appointed position of chair of chartering during that process.

Pamela is a graduate of Tennessee State University, where she received her Bachelor's degree in business administration/management. She also serves as an ambassador for the City of Houston at various industry tradeshows and conferences throughout the US.

A native of Petersburg, Virginia she is the daughter of George and Lessie Ellis. She is also a devoted and proud parent of one son, Christopher.

Karin serves as director of sales for the Gulf South District managing the East Division (Houston & Louisiana). Prior to the UPS Transformation, served as the director of sales when Gulf South consisted of the entire states of Louisiana and Mississippi.

Karin began her career with UPS in November of 1999 in Phoenix, Arizona as an account executive. She held multiple positions within business development including key AE, senior AE, sales support supervisor, PCA supervisor and sales planning & performance supervisor.

In 2004, Karin was promoted to Sales Manager and relocated to Dallas, TX. She rotated into the Sales Operations Manager role for the North TX District in 2006. And in July, 2007 was promoted to Staff level as Director of Sales in the Gulf South District and relocated to New Orleans.

A native of Michigan, Karin now resides in Kenner, Louisiana, with her husband Kenneth Bird. She has a Bachelor's degree in business administration from Western Michigan University. Karin is very active in her community and resides on the board of directors as a member for the World Trade Center in Louisiana.

Karin Stafford Bird

Director of Sales
Gulf South District
UPS

Willie Brown is an assistant store director at HEB. In this role, he is responsible for the daily operations of that location. He oversees all sanitation, safety, and organization of the store, and is also responsible for all operational audits in the store.

Willie came to HEB in January of 2008 after an 11 year career with Home Depot. He spent his last 2 ½ years there as the top store leader.

Willie was accepted into The School Of Retail Leadership Program in 2009. Where he went on to work and train in several stores over a one year period. On April 25th. 2010, Willie graduated from the SORL program. From there he received his first assignment at the Atascocita location where he currently works as the assistant store director.

In his spare time, Willie enjoys weightlifting, watching movies, and spending time with his children.

He is a native of Houston, Texas. Willie is the proud father of a son, Kristoper and daughter, Armani.

Willie Brown

Assistant Store Director
H-E-B

LaTayne Bruce

Corporate Account Executive
Nationwide Insurance

LaTayne Bruce is corporate account executive with Nationwide Insurance. In this role, her focus is to build affinity relationships between member-based organizations and Nationwide Insurance. She joined Nationwide Insurance in 2001 and has been in the insurance industry for more than 20 years.

During her Nationwide tenure, LaTayne has mastered the art of sales and relationship building. As a result, she combines her contagious sense of humor and boundless energy with a keen business acumen. She also speaks to corporate and professional groups, and at universities on sales techniques, relationship building that gives back, and how to reinvent oneself with style and grace.

LaTayne is dedicated to serving the community. She is Texas Black Expo chairman of the board of directors, Houston Citizens Chamber of Commerce vice chairman and Houston Works vice chairman of external affairs.

LaTayne holds a bachelor's degree in business management and Master of Business Administration degree, both from LeTourneau University.

She is a native of Freeport, Illinois, and has two married children, Johnnie Simpson Jr. and Jessica Simpson-Jenkins, who also reside in Houston, Texas.

Robert N. Collier

Managing Shareholder,
Attorney at Law
Collier Hudson PLLC

Robert Collier is an attorney and managing shareholder at Collier Hudson PLLC, focusing on partnership and contract disputes, securities fraud, private equity finance and collections. Robert has served as a clerk for Judge Levi Benton of the 215th Harris County District Court and extern for United States District Court Judge Kenneth Hoyt. He has also clerked for Congressman Bennie Thompson and the U.S. Homeland Security Committee.

Prior to his current position, Robert was an associate at Morgan Stanley and worked for Pricewaterhouse Coopers in the United Kingdom.

In 2010 Robert was selected by the *Houston Business Journal* as a 40 Under 40 honoree. Currently, he serves on the boards of the Houston Business Development Board, Fifth Ward Redevelopment Corporation and the Institute for International Awareness. He is also active with 100 Black Men of Houston and the Houston Word Affairs Council. Recently, Robert was selected by United Way Project Blueprint to be part of its Leadership Class XXX.

Robert earned a bachelor's degree from Millsaps College and juris doctorate degree from Thurgood Marshall School of Law.

B renda Hudson Cooper is vice president and human resources business partner with Amegy Bank. In her role, she functions as a liaison between the commercial lending and retail banking business units and the human resources department.

Brenda received a Bachelor of Arts degree in journalism from Kent State University and a Master of Science degree in human resource management from Houston Baptist University. She also holds a professional in human resources certification and is a member of the Society for Human Resource Management.

A member of Jack and Jill of America Inc., Brenda served as foundation chair of the South Belt Houston chapter for two years. She is an active member of Windsor Village United Methodist Church and a charter member of the Psi Mu Omega Chapter of Alpha Kappa Alpha Sorority, Inc., serving the Pearland/Brazoria County.

Brenda is married to KCOH sports broadcaster Ralph Cooper. They are the proud parents of one daughter, Sydney Taylor Cooper.

Brenda Hudson Cooper

Vice President
Human Resources Business Partner
Amegy Bank N.A.

A s Senior director of corporate administration and shared services IT for Hewlett-Packard (HP), LaTasha Gary leads a global team of IT professionals. LaTasha and her team provide best in class applications and infrastructure for HP's Financial Services, Global Supply Chain Services, and Global Business Services focused on increasing business value and optimizing the company's business effectiveness and workforce.

LaTasha was named Information Technology Senior Management Forum Member of the year in 2009. In 2008, she was presented with the Texas A&M University Distinguished Former Student Award and she was recognized by *Who's Who in Black Houston*. In 2004 LaTasha was named Top Houston Women in Technology by the Association of Women in Computing and in 2002 and she was named Women of Color in Technology All Stars by Career Communications Group.

LaTasha has a Bachelor of Science degree in computer science from Texas A&M University and a Master of Science degree in Computer Science from Howard University.

LaTasha Gary

Senior Director
Corporate Administration and
Shared Services IT
Hewlett-Packard Company

Ulyess Gary

Security Division Manager
Gulf South District
UPS

U lyess Gary is currently the security division manager for the Gulf South District at UPS. His area of responsibility ranges from El Paso, Texas, to Lousiana.

Ulyess's career with UPS started as a loader unloader in metro New York in 1989. In 1990 he joined the Marine Corps Reserves, was deployed to Operation Desert Storm, and returned to UPS upon his release from active duty. Ulyess filled various positions in the security department and was relocated to South Florida in 2004 as a security manager.

In 2005 Ulyess was promoted to security division manager in the South Florida District. In 2009 he was given the additional responsibility of the Hollywood package operation.

Ulyess, who resides in Texas, is married and has two daughters and a son. Ulyess holds a bachelor's degree in organizational management from Manhattan College.

Outside UPS, Ulyess is active in the National Urban Leagues' Black Executive Exchange Program (BEEP) and is a member of the Marine Corps League.

Kenyatta Gibbs

Vice President
Energy Lender
Amegy Bank N.A.

K enyatta Gibbs is a vice president in the Energy Division at Amegy Bank. She has 15 years of experience in finance. Prior to joining Amegy in 2007, she held positions at Credit Agricole, Comerica and JPMorgan Chase.

A board member of the Child Care Council of Greater Houston, Kenyatta is a member of the Women's Energy Network, where she serves on the Outreach Committee that focuses on encouraging high school girls to pursue careers in energy. She is also affiliated with Texas Wall Street Women.

Kenyatta holds a Bachelor of Science degree in finance from Prairie View A&M University and a Master of Business Administration degree from the University of Houston.

DeMonica D. Gladney is counsel for Exxon Mobil Corporation, where she has practiced for 16 years. She began her legal career as a briefing attorney for the Texas 14th Court of Appeals. She received a bachelor of Science degree, cum laude, from Lamar University and a juris doctorate degree, cum laude, from the University of Houston Law Center.

DeMonica serves as chair of the Women Lawyers Division and corporate liaison of the Commercial Law Section of the National Bar Association (NBA) and received the 2010 NBA Presidential Award. She is a former president of the Houston Lawyers Association and chair of the African-American Lawyers Section of the State Bar of Texas and served on the executive board of the Houston Volunteer Lawyers Program. She is a member of the Houston Bar Association, the Corporate Counsel Women of Color, Alpha Kappa Alpha Sorority, Inc. and a life fellow of the Texas Bar Foundation.

DeMonica is an inspirational speaker, poet and the bestselling author of three books, *Identity Theft: Discovering the Real You, Willing to Wait,* and *Reflections from God.*

DeMonica D. Gladney

Attorney at Law
Exxon Mobil Corporation

Monique Graham is the manager of diversity & inclusion at Froedtert Health. She provides expertise in diversity, strategies for staff and community engagement, and creating a culture of inclusion. As a Fortune 100 company's EEO, diversity & inclusion manager, she was responsible for leading, developing and implementing diversity and inclusion strategies, programs and outreach to over 56,000 employees globally.

Monique currently sits on the board for Northcott Neighborhood House and is a member of Girlfriends Inc. She has been involved with numerous community groups such as: Reach for the Stars (organization to raise awareness and prevent teen pregnancy), the Boys and Girls Clubs of America, Junior Achievement, United Negro College Fund, Mosaic partnership, and the White House Initiative for Historically Black Colleges and Universities.

Monique received a Bachelor of Science degree in business administration, a human resource management certificate from Cardinal Stritch University and a certificate in diversity management from the University of Houston.

This Milwaukee native is married to James II, and is a mother of three children which includes a set of twins.

Monique Graham

Manager
Diversity & Inclusion Froedtert Health

Jacqueline Green

Vice President & Banking Center
Manager
Comerica Bank – Texas Market

Jacqueline Green is vice president of Comerica Bank and serves as manager of Comerica's Highway 249 – Louetta Banking Center.

She joined Comerica Bank – Michigan in 1991, where she began her career as a management trainee. She managed several Comerica banking centers in Michigan before relocating to Houston in 2006.

Green has served on the Clay Road Family YMCA board of directors and is involved in numerous other causes that advocate financial literacy, education, mentoring youth, preventing premature babies and breast cancer awareness.

A graduate of Wayne State University in Michigan, Green has a bachelor's degree in accounting.

Jay Griffin

Unit Director, Old Spanish Trail
H-E-B

Jay Griffin, unit director of the Old Spanish Trail H-E-B store in the Houston Division, is responsible for leading day-to-day operations and teamwork among H-E-B partners, as well as ensuring that customers are provided with quality products and outstanding customer service.

Jay has received numerous honors and achievements in diversity, leadership development and community involvement in both Houston and California. He is a member of H-E-B Diversity Council, Rotary Club, Lions Club, NAACP, and Church Without Walls in Houston.

He obtained an associate degree in business administration from Citrus College, followed by a bachelor's degree in business management from Cerritos College.

A native of California, Jay now resides in Houston. He is married to Jan Griffin and the father of four children, Jay Jr., Justin, Devonne, and D.L. He is also the proud grandfather of Devin, Juliana, Brieonna, David Jr., and Emma.

B ruce Harrison is the store director of H-E-B grocery store #012 in Beaumont Texas. In this role he is responsible for developing future leaders and partners for this great establishment. He is also responsible for driving incremental sales and protecting all the financial objectives for H-E-B.

Bruce has also served as the president of Phi Beta Sigma Fraternity, Inc., Iota Iota chapter in 1990. He is also certified in Laubach for Literacy in helping people with reading deficiencies to begin to learn how to read. Bruce received his bachelor's degree in arts and humanities from the University of Louisiana at Lafayette in 1991.

A native of Opelousas, Louisiana, he is the husband of Cynthia Harrison and a very proud father of Bruce II.

Bruce Harrison

Store Director
H-E-B Grocery Store

I nterContinental Houston's director of engineering, Charles Heath, is responsible for maintaining the physical building structure and related assets of the 485-guest room property with 50,000 square feet of meeting space.

In 1991 Charles joined InterContinental Hotels & Resorts, and has since held executive positions in London, Barbados and Puerto Rico.

A member of the Chartered Institution of Building Services Engineers, he holds certifications in electrical engineering.

Charles Heath

Director of Engineering
InterContinental Houston

Moses Horn

Loss Prevention Supervisor
H-E-B

M oses Horn, loss prevention supervisor for H-E-B's Houston and Temple manufacturing, warehousing and transportation facilities. He is accountable for providing physical and corporate security for more than 70,000 H-E-B partners (H-E-B employees), vendors, and contract employees. He is also a HEB corporate ambassador for the Houston Region.

Moses was honored as H-E-B's 2005 Security Partner of the Year. He has received the David Ashworth Community Service Award and originator of a project to provide dinner for kids and their families at the Houston Chapter Ronald McDonald House.

Moses attended Texas A&M University (TAMU) of Kingsville. He was inducted into Texas A&M Sports Hall of Fame in 2009. While attending TAMU he was a team captain and an AP Football First Team All-American in 1986 and 1987. He was also named to the Lone Star Conference Football 1980's All-Decade First Team.

Moses has been married to his wife, Denise, for 11 years. They have one son, Moses J. Horn III.

Larry Johnson

Store Director, Beaumont 1
H-E-B

L arry Johnson, store director for H-E-B Beaumont 1, is responsible for leading the operation of a successful store through great people to achieve maximum return on investment.

Larry actively works in the community to inspire lives and contributes to making a difference. He actively serves on various boards, including food banks, the NAACP, The Young Men's Business League, The Beaumont Chamber of Commerce and Habitat for Humanity, The March of Dimes and Gift of Life. He is also a mentor for Ben's Kids. Larry has been featured numerous times in *The Beaumont Enterprise* as a community advocate.

Within H-E-B, he served as chairman of the 2008 H-E-B Feast of Sharing, UNCF chairman for the Golden Triangle and is director of the Houston Leadership Diversity Council. He has won numerous awards, including the 2000 and 2001 Manager of Excellence Award.

Larry majored in business at Lamar University. He is a native of Beaumont, Texas, and a faithful member of 32 years of Ebenezer Baptist Church.

Larry is a proud and devoted father to Omari Johnson.

Dallas S. Jones

Chief Executive Officer
ELITE Change LLC

D allas S. Jones is the chief executive officer of ELITE Change LLC. Since 2006 ELITE Change has grown to be a nationally recognized firm in the areas of public affairs, strategic communications and business development, with offices in Houston, Texas and Washington, D.C. The organization boasts clients on the national, state and local levels including the NAACP National Voter Fund, numerous local elected officials, and AT&T, where Jones oversees public affairs for 12 states in the Western Region.

Named one of the 40 Power Leaders Under 40 in the country in 2010 by the NAACP, Jones is very active in the community. He serves on the board of the Fourth Ward Redevelopment Authority and Tax Increment Reinvestment Zone. Also, he is active with the Exceptional Men of the Talented Tenth Inc., Express Children's Theatre, MODIFY and the Most Worshipful EM Hunter Grand Lodge of Texas.

Jones is a proud alumnus of Sam Houston State University. He resides in Houston's historic Third Ward with his wife, Angela, and their dog, Ivy.

Winston J. Labbé

Vice President
Commercial Lender
Amegy Bank N.A.

W inston Labbé is a vice president with Amegy Bank, where he works in the community development group as a commercial lender. In addition to lending, he is responsible for community outreach initiatives such as participating on business finance panels, coordinating financial literacy workshops and mentoring grade school students.

An active member of the community, Winston currently sits on the board for several organizations, including the Boy Scouts of America, Texas Business Alliance, The Furniture Bank, and the TSU School of Business Advisory Committee. Winston is also the past recipient of the YMCA's African American Achievers Award. On weekends, Winston volunteers his time with the Youth Ministry at The Fort Bend Church in Sugar Land, Texas.

Winston is a native Houstonian. He received an associate degree in real estate from Houston Community College and a Bachelor of Business Administration degree in finance from Texas Southern University. He is also a U.S. Army veteran, having served four years of active duty.

Winston is married to Tammy and has two children, Sheridan and Winston II.

Waring Lester

District Operations Manager
UPS

Waring Lester is district operations manager at UPS. In 2004 Waring was recognized as on of the top 40 under 40 executives in the Chicago Land Area by *Crain's Chicago Business* magazine.

In April 2006 Waring relocated to San Francisco, California to accept a promotion as the district operations manager for the North California District.

In January 2008, Waring accepted and assignment in the corporate office human resources department as lead facilitator for corporate schools in Provo, Utah. In that role he was responsible for training and developing supervisors and managers. Following his return to the North California District he accepted the assignment as Metro New York District operations manager in October 2008.

In April of 2010 Waring accepted the assignment of district operations manager in Houston, Texas.

A native of Chicago, Illinois, Waring now resides in Houston, Texas. He has a Bachelor of Science degree from National-Louis University.

Obediah Lewis

Unit Director
H-E-B

Obediah "Obe" Lewis is a unit director in H-E-B's Houston Division. In this role, Obe has served the H-E-B located at Old Spanish Trail and Scott Street and the H-E-B located at Beechnut and Beltway 8.

With 18 years of experience in the grocery and retail industries, Obe exhibits an understanding of organization, strategy and technique development, store logistics, local customer needs and the importance of excellent customer service. He has been recognized for his countless efforts in studying the community and surrounding competitors.

Obe is well-respected for his community efforts and has been recognized in various forums, newspapers, and ceremonies. In 2010, he was honored with a proclamation from the City of Houston for all of his volunteer efforts, leadership, and community improvements during his work as manager at Old Spanish Trail and Scott Street.

Obe attended Alabama A&M University, and is a member of the Kappa Alpha Psi Fraternity, Inc..

Obe lives in Cypress with his wife, Erica, and two children, Obediah David and Naomi Gail.

D iane Maben, senior vice president of product management for Amegy Bank, is a product strategist with expertise in innovative product development. With more than 20 years of retail banking experience, she is a dynamic, influential leader and team builder.

Diane is directly responsible for providing leadership to the bank's product management team. In her role, she establishes the product strategy for the retail and small business teams to ensure alignment with key business initiatives. Her team is accountable for new product development, pricing and profitability, as well staying abreast of the competitive landscape.

Born in Memphis, Tennessee, Diane moved to Houston shortly after completing her undergraduate degree at Smith College in Northampton, Massachusetts. She received a Bachelor of Arts degree in economics.

Diane Maben

Senior Vice President
Product Management
Amegy Bank N.A.

C harnissa "Nikki" Parker is the vice president of the Windermere Lakes Banking Center for Comerica Bank N.A. As a banking center Manager she is responsible to motivate, inform, educate, develop, and coach banking center staff to ensure all objectives, financial goals, and service standards are met. Nikki is also responsible for maximize sales and profitability within the branch as well.

Nikki has over 14 years of experience in the financial service industry. She has been a banking center manager for over 10 years. Nikki has also been awarded multiple awards for Outstanding Customer Service, and she has also successfully passed all banking center audits in her career.

Nikki received a Bachelor of Arts degree from McNeese State University in 1997. She also received her certificate of management in banking in 2002, and also holds her NASD Series 6 Security License, and her Life, Health, and Annuity Licenses for the states of both Louisiana and Texas.

A native of Lake Charles, Louisiana, Nikki is the wife of Derrick Parker and the proud mother of three daughters, Jenelle, Madison, and Kaylee.

Charnissa "Nikki" Parker

Vice President
Windermere Lakes Banking Center
Comerica Bank N.A.

Michael Pearson

Senior Vice President
Real Estate Lender
Amegy Bank N.A.

Michael Pearson is a senior vice president and real estate lender at Amegy Bank. In his role in the not-for-profit lending group, he is responsible for providing financial products, services and trusted advice to tax-exempt, not-for-profit clients and prospects of the bank.

With 32 years of banking experience, Michael served as a credit officer in the global oil and gas division at JPMorgan Chase, as well as a relationship manager with other financial institutions for healthcare and oil and gas industries.

Michael holds a certified financial planner designation and is a U.S. Treasury Department enrolled agent. He earned a bachelor's degree in business management from Fisk University and a master's degree from Pepperdine University.

Michael is the board of directors' treasurer for the Houston Area Urban League, a trustee for The Battleship Texas Foundation and is a member of the Art Colony Association Artist Support Committee. He is also on the local and state boards of the Risk Management Association (RMA) and serves on the RMA National Leaders Conference Committee.

Michael is active in cultural arts, performing arts, academic and social service communities in Houston.

Stephen Pope

Showtime Marketing Manager
H-E-B

Stephen Pope, showtime marketing manager for H-E-B, is accountable for the operation and execution of H-E-B's Showtime Demo Program, where customers are offered cooking information and food sampling. His daily responsibilities include training partners, delivering sales results and communicating goals and sales initiatives. The program has enabled H-E-B to differentiate itself from competitors by offering a unique, interactive shopping experience.

Stephen has worked with H-E-B Showtime since its inception in 2006. Prior to this, he graduated from H-E-B's School of Retail Leadership and served in several operations positions as store director.

Prior to joining H-E-B, Stephen served in the U.S. Air Force, retiring after 24 years of service. His service to the country has enabled him to travel around the world to include positions at the Pentagon, in Germany and Australia to name a few.

Stephen received a bachelor's degree in business management from Park University. He is currently attending Tulane University working towards a Master of business administration degree. He is currently an active member of Brentwood Baptist Church.

Kim Prince, a human resources manager for H-E-B, is responsible for consulting multiple store locations on a myriad of issues including but not limited to the following: employee relations, performance management, and policy/procedure compliance. Along with these responsibilities, Kim oversees the Recognition and Health/Wellness Programs for the Houston Division.

Kim's 20 years with H-E-B have allowed her to gain retail experience as a department and store manager, which provide a solid foundation for her current role.

In addition to her work activities, Kim assists her church, Reflections of Christ's Kingdom (ROCK), by serving on the Finance Committee and working in the church's book/media store. Kim is also a court-appointed child advocate through Child Advocates, Inc. Through this organization, she serves and supports children in the greater Houston area who are in the foster care system.

Kim, a native of Dallas, graduated from the University of Texas with a bachelor's degree in management in May 1990. She completed her Master of Busines administration degree from the University of Phoenix in April 2004. In her spare time, she enjoys traveling, reading, and attending football and basketball games.

Kimberly Prince

Human Resources Manager
H-E-B Houston Division

Frederick Richardson Jr. is a unit director for H-E-B, and is responsible for successful retail operations of his unit. Frederick has 17 years of grocery retail experience. He maintains the successful operations by offering personable customer service, engaging with his partners, staying involved in community events and being a positive role model advocate for healthy eating, education, health and fitness.

The Texas Black Employees Association and Angel Faces, Inc. has honored Frederick for his outstanding service and dedication in the South Oak Cliff community. He was also recognized with the Texas Lifetime Community Service Award from Texas Youth Against Drugs and Crime in Houston along with other past recognition in the Dallas and Houston communities.

Frederick attended Lamar University and Galveston College. He has a certificate of completion for the complete manager course from Cornell University.

Frederick in the most recent years has found a new church home at Grace Community Church and a native of Galveston he is still a member of St Augustines church. Frederick and his wife, Precious of 13 years, reside in Houston with their family.

Frederick Richardson Jr.

Unit Director
H-E-B

Lacey Dalcour Salas

Senior Public Affairs Specialist
H-E-B

As a senior public affairs specialist for H-E-B Houston, Lacey Dalcour Salas is responsible for managing numerous community outreach and public affairs initiatives at H-E-B.

She oversees special events and signature community programs that highlight H-E-B's philanthropic giving in the community; including the H-E-B Holiday Parade and the Feast of Sharing, amongst many others. Lacey plans and executes H-E-B new store opening strategies within the Houston region, and serves as a daily point-of-contact for in-store community coordinators.

Lacey is a member of the H-E-B Houston Diversity Council where she manages the office of market place co-chair. Additionally, she was awarded the H-E-B Woman of Distinction for the Houston corporate office in 2011.

She is a dedicated member of the Leukemia and Lymphoma Society, and has been honored as a Woman of the Year Candidate for 2011.

Prior to her time at H-E-B, Lacey assisted with marketing and game operations within the athletics department at Texas State University and worked in Season Ticket Services for Spurs Sports and Entertainment.

Lacey earned a Bachelor of Arts degree in mass communication – public relations from Texas State University.

Kevins Scott

Store Director
H-E-B Houston Division

As store director, Kevins Scott leads the company's largest retail grocery store inside the 610 loop of Houston. During his 30 years in the grocery business, Scott gained an understanding of many cultures in the area. He provides a diverse assortment of goods and services to his customers. The selection of African-American, Hispanic, Asian and Salvadorian products are first class in the market his store serves. He aims to provide a one-stop shopping experience for every customer.

Awarded a scholarship to the University of Missouri where he completed two years towards his degree, Scott attended Cameron School of Business where he received a bachelor's degree in business administration, and is a member of Omega Psi Phi Fraternity, Inc.

Most of his values that he still has today were taught to him by his mother (deceased), and father, who is a retired Baptist minister in Oklahoma. Kevins and wife, Marilyn, live in Spring, Texas. He has two children, Heather, a graduate of the University of Houston and Kevins, a student at San Jacinto College.

K eisha Wilson Tanner is the area support engineering team leader for the Holstein Facility in BP's Gulf of Mexico Production Performance Unit. She leads a team of facilities, operations and integrity management engineers directly supporting day-to-day operations of an offshore platform.

In 1995 Keisha was commended by the Georgia House of Representatives. As the BP African American Network's Houston Chapter co-leader, she focuses on increasing the representation, inclusion and advancement of African Americans. She is also BP's Campus Champion for Georgia Tech. In this role, Keisha is responsible for setting a recruiting strategy and budget to attract and hire top quartile undergraduate engineers.

Keisha is a member of Alpha Kappa Alpha Sorority, Inc., the National Society of Black Engineers, the Society of Women Engineers and the Houston Livestock and Rodeo Black Heritage Committee.

Keisha received a bachelor's degree in chemical engineering from Georgia Tech in 1995. A native of Nicholls, Georgia, Keisha is the proud mother of one daughter, Chelsea. Her hobbies include tennis, skiing and dancing. She is a member of Lakewood Church.

Keisha Wilson Tanner

Engineering Team Leader
BP Exploration and Production, Inc.

T ravis Torrence is a senior associate at Fulbright & Jaworski L.L.P., where he represents creditors and debtors in bankruptcy and insolvency-related matters. Travis was honored by *Texas SuperLawyers* as a Rising Star and served as secretary of the bankruptcy section of the Houston Bar Association. Travis is currently a member of Fulbright's Diversity Committee and the Houston office's Recruiting Committee. Previously, Travis was a law clerk for the Honorable Edward C. Prado, circuit judge for the United States Court of Appeals for the Fifth Circuit.

Travis graduated from Yale Law School in 2005 and was a director of the Yale Nonprofit Organizations Clinic and treasurer of the Black Law Students Association. He was also an editor of the *Yale Journal on Regulation*.

Travis received an undergraduate degree, summa cum laude, in communication and political science from Tulane University, where he was president of the Zeta Psi Fraternity and the Order of Omega. He was also vice president of Omicron Delta Kappa and a member of the Tulane College Honor Board.

Travis Alexander Torrence

Senior Associate, Attorney at Law
Fulbright & Jaworski L.L.P.

Eli Warren

General Manager
H-E-B Houston Division

Eli Warren, general manager at the Gulfgate, Houston #540 H-E-B store, creates a team environment where H-E-B employees are trained and developed to ensure customers are provided quality products and superior customer service. His duties include maintaining all federal, state and company regulation standards for product freshness and safety. He is also accountable for hiring, training, development and partner retention.

Eli is a Desert Storm veteran that spent 10 years in the U.S. Air Force, before joining H-E-B in February of 2000. He was the first Houston Food & Drug Pantry partner to graduate from the H-E-B School of Retail Leadership (SORL).

Eli has been awarded several honors with H-E-B, including H-E-B's Hal Collett Great People, the David Ashworth Community Service and the Harvey Mabry Excellence in Management awards.

Eli, a native Houstonian, earned a Master of Business Administration degree from Hawaii Pacific University and a bachelor's degree from Wayland Baptist University. He and his wife, Felicia, have four children, Shayla, Emily, Elexis and AJ. Eli is also a grandfather to Kayla. He attributes his successes to his father, Michael C. Warren.

Tammy Watson

Store Director
H-E-B

After serving time in the military, Tammy earned her Bachelor of Business Administration degree from the University of Houston. She joined H-E-B in January 2002, and was accepted into the SORL program in February 2002. After simultaneously completing SORL and obtaining her Master of Business Administration degree from Sam Houston State University, she assisted in the grand opening of the Bay Colony H-E-B.

Tammy served as assistant store director at the Kingwood H-E-B starting in April of 2005 where she was promoted to store director in November of 2005. While serving at Kingwood, Tammy received the store nomination for Excellence in Management in 2007. In May of 2007, Tammy was selected as the Center Store Leader for Vintage Market. There she also served as the perishable director. In August 2009, Tammy was promoted to store director at the Cleveland H-E-B, where she currently serves.

Tammy has also served as the workplace chair on the Diversity Council from September of 2005 through September 2007.

L ionel White is the senior manager of global marketing operations for Hewlett-Packard Company (HP). In this role, White directs analytical resources and processes to deliver performance insights, return on investment assessments and facilitates marketing results improvement initiatives within the Enterprise Hardware Division.

White has held key roles in HP's U.S. Affinity Marketing Operations, Global PC Business Planning, and Global Small Business Market Strategy and Planning. His contributions within HP led to him being awarded the HP Key Talent Leadership Award, an award where selection is limited to the top 1 percent of eligible employees.

Prior to joining HP, White was based in Chicago as a management consultant with A.T. Kearney and in Cincinnati as an outbound logistics manager with Procter & Gamble.

Lionel earned a Master of Business Administration degree from Northwestern University and is enthusiastically married with four children.

Lionel White

Senior Manager
Global Marketing Operations
Hewlett-Packard Company

E lijah J. Williams is a contracting officer at NASA in the Exploration Systems Procurement Office, contract analysis and changes team, in support of several key agency initiatives to develop the next generation space transportation vehicle and to develop commercial industry capabilities to deliver cargo to low earth orbit.

A native of New Orleans, Louisiana, Elijah earned a Bachelor of Science degree in business administration, with a concentration in management, from Xavier University of Louisiana and a Master of Public Administration degree, with a concentration in public policy from Texas Southern University.

In addition, Elijah serves as president of the Houston Area Urban League Young Professionals and is a member of the board of directors of the Houston Area Urban League. He is a member of Alpha Phi Alpha Fraternity, Inc. and Wheeler Avenue Baptist Church.

In Elijah's free time he enjoys playing his drum set, listening to music, playing with his dog, participating in various sporting activities and traveling.

Elijah J. Williams

Contracting Officer
Johnson Space Center
NASA

Kimberly J. Williams

Chief Administrative Officer
Capital Programs
Metropolitan Transit Authority of
Harris County

K imberly J. Williams is chief administrative officer of Capital Programs for the Metropolitan Transit Authority of Harris County (METRO). Williams oversees finance, real estate, community and business outreach and media relations for the Capital Programs area.

Williams is part of the management team implementing METRO's expansion of light rail and transit improvements throughout the Houston region. Williams is president of the Houston Chapter of the Conference of Minority Transportation Officials (COMTO), which is the only association dedicated to advancement of minorities in all modes of transportation. She serves on the boards of Houston Citizens Chamber of Commerce, Midtown Redevelopment Authority and is a member of Delta Sigma Theta Sorority, Inc. Prior to METRO, she served as vice president of external relations for Texas Southern University.

In 2010, Williams was named COMTO's Emerging Leader of the Year, Top 40 under 40 by *rolling out* magazine and a member of Leadership Houston Class XXIX.

Williams is a graduate of Howard University and Wayne State Law School where she served as survey editor of the *Wayne Law Review*. She is the proud mother of one daughter, MacKenzie.

Spring G. Williams

Gulf South District Air Manager
UPS

S pring G. Williams is the District Air Manager for the Gulf South District. Spring has the responsibility for the Houston, New Orleans, Shreveport and Lafayette Gateways.

Spring started her career with UPS as a package driver in the Tulsa Facility, Oklahoma district. She was promoted to the management ranks in package operations. Spring was promoted and relocated to package division manager in the Southeast Texas District. She was the package division manger responsible for beta testing of four major projects within the organization. In 2006, she rotated from a package division manager to her current assignment as the air division manager.

Spring is very active in her role as a mother of two adult children, Aric Gaines and Sparkle Gaines and three wonderful grandchildren. Spring is deeply involved in her church, Payne Cathedral of Faith A.M.E. She is a licensed minister as well as volunteers with various youth groups.

D ebbie Wilson is the director of human resources for H-E-B in Houston. She is responsible for the human resource function for the Houston Food Division, which consist of more than 14,000 Partners.

In this role, she works collaboratively with company leadership on strategic and succession planning, workforce management and employee development.

Debbie has worked in the human resources industry for more than 12 years. She joined H-E-B in April of 2006.

In her spare time, Debbie enjoys volunteering. She is a strong supporter of UNCF, American Heart Association, March of Dimes and Junior Achievement. She also worked successfully with the YMCA of Greater Houston to help bring affordable fitness program options to H-E-B Partners.

Debbie received her Bachelor of Arts degree from the University of Houston. In 2003, she received her professional certification in human resources. She is also an active member of the Society of Human Resources.

A native of Milwaukee, Wisconsin, Debbie is the proud mother of one, Jillvonni.

Debbie Wilson
Director of Human Resources
H-E-B Houston Division

COMMON GROUND.

While we may come from different backgrounds and have different points of view, experiences and ideas, we're all in this together.

Our communities grow stronger when we share common goals and dreams.

At Comerica Bank, we proudly support Who's Who in Black Houston and everything you do to strengthen the community.

Comerica Bank

comerica.com

Houston's
AFRICAN-AMERICAN
DOCTORS

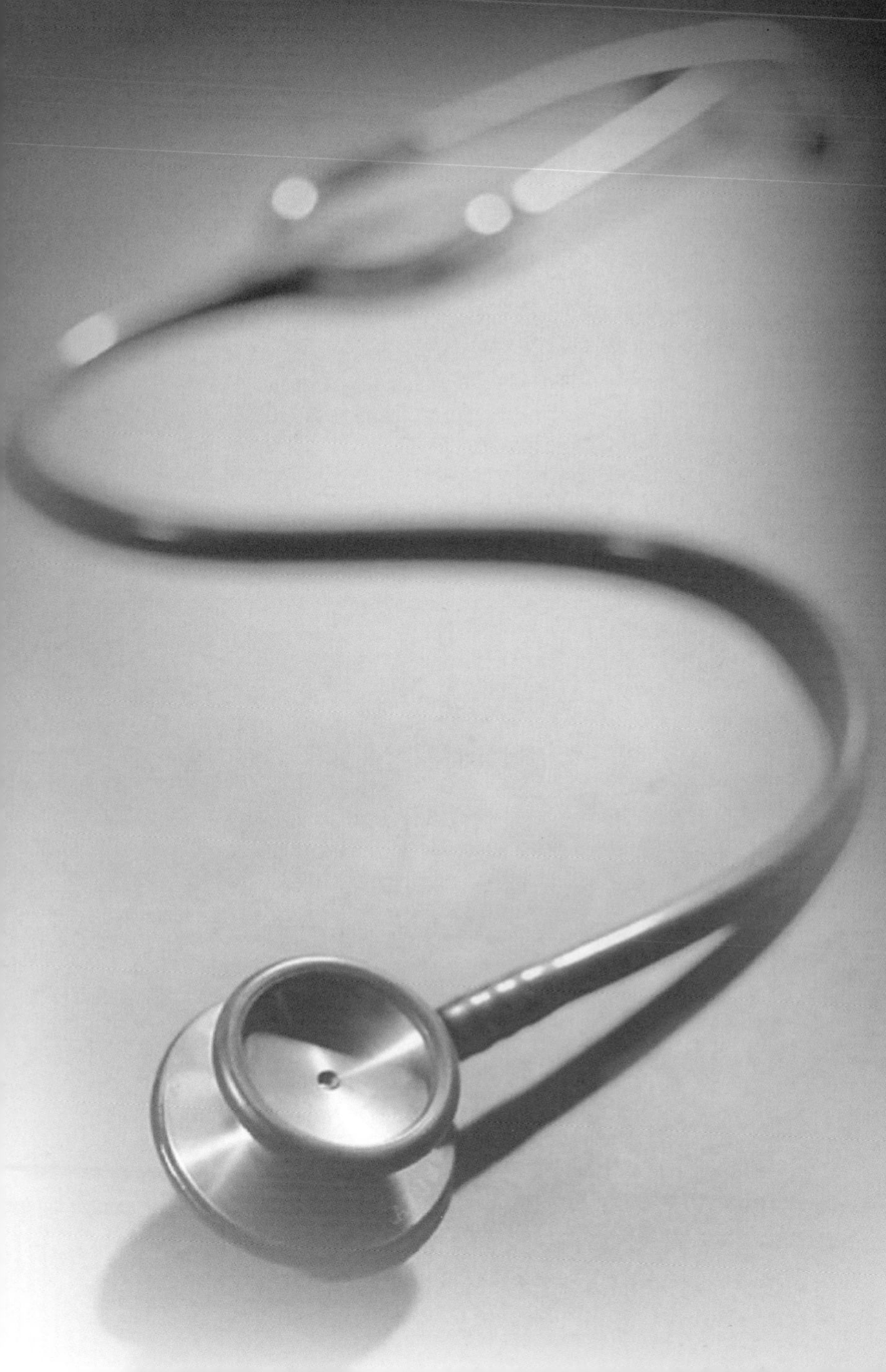

PIONEER

COMPASSIONATE

PRECEPTOR

DEDICATED

SALUBRIOUS

RESEARCHER

METICULOUS

APOTHECARY

SPECIALIST

DOCTORS

Regina A. Bailey, M.D.

Emergency Medicine Resident Physician
Baylor College of Medicine

Dr. John E. Codwell III

Owner & Medical Director
Codwell Family Foot Center, PA

Dr. Regina A. Bailey has an undergraduate degree in molecular biology from Hampton University, a juris doctorate degree from Georgetown University, a Doctor of Medicine degree from George Washington University and a Master in Health Law degree from the University of Houston. She is currently an emergency medicine resident physician at the Baylor College of Medicine and primarily works out of Ben Tub Hospital.

Prior to attending medical school she was a patent litigation attorney in Washington, D.C. She is licensed to practice law in Washington, D.C., Texas and also before the U.S. Supreme Court.

Regina has done biomedical research at the National Institutes of Health, the Yale University School of Medicine, the Stanford University School of Medicine and the Maryland Anderson Cancer Center. She has published multiple articles in the biomedical research and health law fields.

During law school, Regina was a NFL cheerleader for the Washington Redskins. She is now a member of the NFL Alumni Association and the Science Cheerleaders performance troupe. Earlier this year, Regina was crowned Ms. Woodlands and was crowned Ms. Texas United Southern States.

Dr. John Codwell III, owner and medical director of Codwell Family Foot Center, PA, is a graduate of the Ohio College of Podiatric Medicine. He completed his podiatric residency training at the Hunter-Holmes McGuire Veteran's Administration Hospital in Richmond, Virginia.

Although he specializes in medical and surgical treatment of the foot and ankle including sports related issues, Codwell has a special interest in diabetic foot care. He frequently lectures on the prevention and management of diabetes. He also is very active on many hospital and surgery center staffs, where he provides medical and surgical care to patients with a variety of foot and ankle problems.

Codwell is board certified and is an active member of the American Podiatric Medical Associations, Texas Podiatric Medical Association and is a national officer of the National Podiatric Medical Association.

Codwell is married to Wendy Turner Codwell, an attorney, and is the proud father of three sons, John IV, Reid and Austin.

Dr. Alison Scott Cuillier

Owner
Cosmetic & Implant Dentist
Lasting Impressions Dental Group, PLLC

Paul J. James, M.D.

Surgeon
Metropolitan Houston Surgery Associates, Pllc

Since 2002, Dr. Alison Scott Cuillier and her team of dental professionals have served more than 5,500 patients at her practice located in Houston's Midtown/Museum District.

A Houston native, Alison received an undergraduate degree at the University of North Texas and a graduate degree at the University of Texas-Dental Branch, Houston. She is a member of Delta Sigma Theta Sorority, Inc., the Eco Dentistry Association, the National Dental Association, the American Academy of Cosmetic Dentistry and is one of the founding members of the Christian Business Outreach. Her volunteer efforts include international dentistry mission trips, community health fairs, public school awareness and 5K runs for various causes.

In 2010 she was recognized by *rolling out* magazine as one of the Top 25 Women of Houston, and awarded with the Pinnacle Award by Houston Citizens Chamber of Commerce. In 2009 she was featured in *Vogue* magazine, and in 2007 she was named Houston's Top Dentist.

She is married to Joseph Cuillier Jr., has a son, Julian, three bonus children, Christen, Joseph III, and Sydney and two bonus grandchildren, Jaylen and Jace.

Paul J. James M.D., specializes in general and laparoscopic surgery, and has more than 20 years of experience and is always dedicated to providing comprehensive and quality patient care. From one-on-one personalized consultations to attentive follow-up care, James is actively involved in every facet of treatment. He strongly believes in educating his patients and ensuring that they have a clear understanding of the procedures and the end results.

He received an undergraduate degree from Texas Southern University, and later attended Meharry Medical College School of Medicine in Nashville, Tennessee, where he received a Doctorate of Medicine degree. He then completed his general surgery residency at the St Joseph Hospital in Houston, Texas. James is a fellow of the American College of Surgeons. He is also a member of numerous professional organizations such as American Medical Association, Texas Medical Foundation and Houston Medical Forum.

He has received numerous awards and honors including graduating, cum laude, from Texas Southern University.

Sheila Jenkins, Ph.D.

Psychologist
Sheila Jenkins, Ph.D. & Associates

Melanie Mencer-Parks, M.D.

President
Synergy Medical and Wellness Group

Dr. Sheila Jenkins is a private practice psychologist in Houston, Texas. Since beginning her private practice in 1992, she has soared to become one of the most highly regarded psychologists in Houston. As a highly trained health provider, Jenkins is frequently called on by various media outlets to discuss the issues affecting our nation. The only minority to be elected president of the Houston Psychological Association, she later served as president of the Texas Psychological Foundation, a nonprofit organization that provides funding to Texas communities.

Jenkins is a member of Delta Sigma Theta Sorority, Inc. and served as president of the Suburban Houston – Fort Bend Alumnae Chapter from 2004 to 2006. In 2007 she was recognized as one of the most accomplished Americans in the 61st edition of Marquis *Who's Who in America.*

Jenkins earned a Bachelor of Science degree in psychology from the University of Houston in 1985 and a Doctor of Philosophy degree in psychology from the University of Georgia in 1992. Additionally, she completed postdoctoral training at the Houston Veterans Administration Hospital before entering private practice.

Dr. Melanie Mencer-Parks is a well-respected family medicine physician in Houston. She is president of Synergy Medical and Wellness Group where she and her associates treat a myriad of medical conditions including weight loss management. She graduated from Xavier University in New Orleans and from Meharry Medical College in Nashville, Tennessee. She then did her residency training at University of Texas at Houston, where she served as chief resident her last year.

Mencer-Parks has received numerous awards for outstanding achievement in academics and teaching. In 2004 she started her own private practice in the museum district in Houston. In 2005, 2006 and 2007 she was voted and highlighted as one of the Top Doctors in Houston which appeared in *H magazine.*

Currently serving as vice-chair for the Family Practice section of the National Medical Association, Mencer-Parks is a member of the Houston Medical Forum, American Medical Association, Texas Medical Association and Delta Sigma Theta Sorority, Inc.

Originally from Baton Rouge, Louisiana, Mencer-Parks is a wife and mother to three awesome children.

Dr. Sherri Sandifer

Pediatrician
Texas Children's Pediatric Associates

Yvonne S. Thomas, D. M. D.

Partner
Baytown Gentle Dental Center

A native Houstonian, Dr. Sherri Sandifer has been a pediatrician with Texas Children's Pediatric Associates (TCPA), since 2002. She has been a member of the executive committees of Houston Northwest Hospital, the FM1960 Pediatric Center and TCPA. Sandifer served as pediatric department chair at Houston Northwest Hospital and chair of TCPA's Quality Improvement Committee. She is also on the board of directors of M.D. Anderson Cancer Center's Chaplaincy Fund.

After graduating, cum laude, from The Kinkaid School, Sandifer earned both a bachelor's degree in psychology and a medical degree with honors from Yale University. She then completed pediatric residency training at Baylor College of Medicine in Houston.

Sherri is also an accomplished singer/songwriter. She has released her debut album entitled *Loverevolution,* which was produced by Grammy award winner Dru Castro. The album's first single entitled *Don't Call Me* has spent several weeks in the top 10 on Billboard's hot R&B/hip-hop singles sales chart.

Dr. Yvonne S. Thomas is a general dentist and spent the first part of her career in private practice in The Bronx, New York. In 1997 she decided to move to the warmer climate in Texas and has been serving the Baytown community at Baytown Gentle Dental Center. Thomas is dedicated to advancing her skills in order to provide the latest techniques in dentistry and outstanding treatment to her patients.

Thomas participates in many community activities, locally and out of town, spreading the word about dental health. Her latest endeavor has taken her to Haiti where she took part in a medical mission trip to help the less fortunate citizens of Haiti.

Thomas graduated from Pace University, New York, with a Bachelor of Science degree in biology and then entered Fairleigh Dickinson University College of Dental Medicine in Hackensack, New Jersey, where she attained her Doctor of Dental Medicine degree in 1985.

Houston's
ACADEMIA

TEACH

ELEVATE

INSPIRE

COACH

CHALLENGE

MENTOR

SUCEED

VALUE

ENLIGHTEN

Dr. O. Felix Ayadi

Interim Associate Dean
Jesse H. Jones School of Business
Texas Southern University

Dr. O. Felix Ayadi is currently the interim associate dean of the Jesse H. Jones School of Business at Texas Southern University (TSU). He is the JPMorgan Chase endowed chair and professor of finance, publishing more than 65 refereed articles in several academic journals. He teaches finance courses to both graduate and undergraduate students and assists the dean in the school's administration.

Ayadi is listed in *Marquis Who's Who in America* and *Who's Who* Among *America's Teachers*. He is the 2009 recipient of the International Service Award at TSU, the Outstanding Service Award winner from the faculty senate of Fayetteville State University from 1999 through 2001 and the Pee Dee Newspaper Group - Times Upstate Newspaper Positive Image Award in 1996. Ayadi was a Nissan fellow in finance in 1994 and in 1989 he won both the United States Achievement Academy Award and was named an All American Scholar.

Ayadi received a doctorate degree in finance from the University of Mississippi.

Miron P. Billingsley

Associate Vice President of Student Affairs
Prairie View A&M University

Miron P. Billingsley is the associate vice president for student affairs at Prairie View A&M University, where he directs the wide-ranging operations for the Office of Student Affairs, including student activities and leadership, outreach and career services, intramural and recreational sports, judicial services, special programs and testing and diagnostic services.

Billingsley's career in higher education has provided a wealth of experience in dealing with the needs and support of students. Before joining PVAMU, he served as the vice president of student affairs at Arkansas Baptist College, where he managed student affairs, development and programming. Previously, he served as adjunct professor of communications in the Tavis Smiley School of Communications at Texas Southern University.

An advocate for students and learning, Billingsley has also served as the director of training and development for PeopleSoft at the University of Houston and has worked as the director of public relations and marketing at Langston University.

Nelson Bowman, III is the director of development at Prairie View A&M University. As the chief development officer, he is responsible for managing major gift prospects, donor stewardship initiatives and the university's internal school-based fundraising program.

Bowman has presented on the topic of fundraising at black colleges and universities at several major conferences. He is also the co-author of a new book, *Historically Black Colleges and Universities: An Overview* and a forthcoming book, *Fundraising at Black Colleges*. Notably, Bowman oversaw the successful completion of the University's first capital campaign of $30 million.

A Houston native, Bowman joined PVAMU in 2005 after 15 years in corporate management. He has completed formal development training at The Fund Raising School. In 2006, he received a certificate in fundraising management.

The Morehouse graduate earned a bachelor's degree in Business Management and is a member of several professional organizations, including the Association of Fundraising Professionals, the Council for the Advancement and Support of Education (CASE), Thurgood Marshall College Fund's National Alumni Council.

Nelson Bowman, III

Director of Development
Prairie View A&M University

Dr. Lauretta Byars is the vice president of student affairs and institutional advancement. She is responsible for student activities and leadership, development, student judicial services, career services, intramurals and the university's All Faiths Chapel. She has more than 30 years of experience in higher education, community outreach and diversity.

As vice president, Byars links entities within the University to local, state and national agencies to maximize the use of resources for improving education, health, socio-economic and cultural well-being of the citizens of the state.

Byars provides leadership in promoting the university's services and programs that address some of Texas' most critical needs. She is the leader of numerous key areas within the university, including governmental affairs, affirmative action and equal opportunity, public relations, service-learning, multicultural affairs and continuing education.

Before settling in Texas, Byars worked in Kentucky for 32 years in the areas of teaching, research, diversity initiatives, community outreach, faculty development and administration. She received her bachelor's from Morehead State University and master's and doctorate degrees from the University of Kentucky.

Lauretta F. Byars, Ed.D.

Vice President of Student Affairs
and Institutional Relations
Prairie View A&M University

Charleta Guillory, M.D.

Associate Professor of Pediatrics
Baylor College of Medicine

Dr. Charleta Guillory is an associate professor of pediatrics at Baylor College of Medicine and associate director of level II nurseries at Texas Children's Hospital. Her primary interests are decreasing infant mortality and morbidity.

Guillory was a recipient of a Robert Wood Johnson Health Policy Fellowship Award from The Institute of Medicine of the National Academy of Sciences for Outstanding Health Science Professionals to promote health policy legislation and programs. Her leadership in advocacy efforts and in community-based initiatives led to her receiving the National March of Dimes Award of Distinction and the American Academy of Pediatrics Special Achievement Award for expanding the Texas Newborn Screening Program.

Guillory earned a Bachelor of Science degree from the University of Southwestern Louisiana, her Doctor of Medicine degree from Louisiana State University (LSU) Medical School, completed her pediatric residency at LSU and the University of Colorado, and received her postdoctoral training in neonatal-perinatal medicine at Baylor College of Medicine. She is board-certified in pediatrics and neonatal-perinatal medicine.

She is the proud mother of a Hampton University graduate, Yohance Turk.

Allan D. Headley, Ph.D.

Dean of Graduate Studies & Research
Professor of Chemistry
Texas A&M University-Commerce

Dr. Allan Headley is dean of graduate studies and research and professor of chemistry at Texas A&M University-Commerce (A&M-C). He provides leadership to ensure that all research activities are in compliance with federal regulations and are of the highest standards. He also ensures that all graduate programs are of the highest quality. He has developed various partnerships with different institutions and industries, and he continues to be instrumental in the development of various science, technology, engineering and math (STEM) alliances to increase graduate enrollment, diversity and retention throughout the university.

Before joining A&M-C, Headley was an associate dean of the graduate school and also a professor of chemistry at Texas Tech University. While there, he concentrated on recruiting efforts that resulted in increased graduate enrollment, especially among under-represented students.

Headley received a bachelor's degree in chemistry from Columbia Union College in Maryland and a Doctor of Philosophy degree in chemistry from Howard University, followed by postdoctoral research at the University of California, Irvine.

Headley is married to Fay Keane-Headley and they are the proud parents of two children, Micah and Jahmela.

D r. Samoan Johnson is an assistant professor and psychologist. She provides clinical services to children and adults in acute distress at the University of Texas-Harris County Psychiatric Center, and conducts research and supervises graduate students and residents.

She serves on the board of directors of the Julia C. Hester House, the Family Services of Greater Houston and the Houston Psychological Association. She serves on the advisory boards of the Systems of Hope and the Interface Samaritan Counseling Centers. Johnson is president-elect of the Houston Psychological Association, past president of the Houston Association of Black Psychologists and an alumna of the United Way Leadership Program.

In 2005, 2007 and 2008, Johnson was named Houston's Top 100 Young Professionals in *H Texas* Magazine. In 2008 she was named as one of Houston's Women on the Move in *D Mars* Magazine. She is a member of Alpha Kappa Alpha Sorority, Inc., and the Links, Inc.

She received a bachelor's degree from Dillard University, a master's degree from Loyola University in Chicago and a doctoral degree from the University of Houston.

Dr. Samoan C. Johnson

Assistant Professor
Department of Psychiatry & Behavioral Sciences
University of Texas Medical School Houston

D r. Danny R. Kelley is the dean of the Marvin D. and June Samuel Brailsford College of Arts and Sciences. He is responsible for the university's largest academic unit. Prior to this appointment Kelley, served as head of the music department and oversaw the department of music and theatre. He also was a professor of piano.

Kelley has performed at the John F. Kennedy Center for the Performing Arts in Washington, D. C., the Houston Museum of Fine Arts and in several different concert venues throughout the Caribbean. In 1994, he toured Germany, performing six concerts at sold out venues. Kelly performed as soloist in Houston's famed Jones Hall in 2001.

Currently, he is a musician at St. Francis Episcopal Church on Piney Point Road. Kelley is active in various community affairs, serving on the first board of directors for the Cynthia Woods Mitchell Pavilion, a major outdoor concert amphitheater in the Woodlands, Texas. He served as president of the Regional Arts Center in Tomball, was a board advisor to the Houston Symphony and a member of the board of directors for the Houston Ebony Opera Guild.

Dr. Danny R. Kelley

Dean
Marvin D. and June Samuel
Brailsford College of Arts and Sciences

Christi A. Landry

Public Relations Specialist
Prairie View A&M University

Christi A. Landry is Public Relations Specialist for Prairie View A&M University. Tasked with promoting notable events, individual excellence and outstanding achievements, Landry serves as the point of contact for publicizing PVAMU's impact on the nation. She works closely with students, faculty, staff and administrators to creating publications, press releases and news stories that showcase excellence in the areas of teaching, research and service.

In 2006, Landry was recognized by the Louisiana Press Association for her reporting during Hurricanes Katrina and Rita. She arrived at PVAMU in 2008, serving as the communications specialist for the Cooperative Agricultural Research Center within the College of Agriculture and Human Sciences.

Landry lends her talents to numerous projects and initiatives, including The Chat Room, an internet radio show. She is also proud to serve as a mentor to many of the students she serves at the University.

Landry received her Bachelor of Arts degree in Mass Communications – Print Journalism from Southern University and A&M College and plans to pursue a Master of Business Administration. She is a member of the National Association of Black Journalists and Delta Sigma Theta Sorority.

Dr. Michael L. McFrazier

Dean & Vice Provost
for Academic Affairs
Prairie View A&M University
Northwest Houston Center

Dr. Michael L. McFrazier, a native of Paris, Texas, is vice provost for academic affairs and dean of the Prairie View A&M University Northwest Houston Center. He holds a Bachelor of Music Education, a Master of Music –Vocal Performance and a Master of Science in Education from Baylor University. He received his Doctorate in Educational Administration from the University of Arkansas, Fayetteville.

Dr. McFrazier joined the faculty at Prairie View A&M University in 1998. He holds the rank of associate professor. Previously, he served as chair of the PVAMU Southern Association of Colleges and Schools, Commission on Colleges Reaffirmation of Accreditation team and was instrumental in developing the Ph.D. Program in educational leadership in the Whitlowe R. Green College of Education.

McFrazier has received numerous honors and is affiliated with numerous organizations including Texas Council of Chief Academic Officers; Leadership Northwest Houston; Research Association for Minority Professors; Prairie View A&M University Men's Leadership Council (founder); Golden Key Honor Society; Phi Kappa Phi Honor Society and Alpha Phi Alpha Fraternity Inc.

Dr. McFrazier currently serves as the minister of music at The Church Without Walls in Houston.

D r. Shirlette Glover Milton is assistant dean for student services, director of pre-health professions programs and associate professor of pharmaceutical chemistry in the College of Pharmacy and Health Sciences at Texas Southern University. She directs activities to recruit and assist over 600 students in pre-health professions programs. She oversees student service activities for five undergraduate programs and the Doctor of Pharmacy program.

Dr. Milton received a bachelor's degree in pharmacy from Texas Southern University, a master's degree in pharmaceutical sciences from the University of Texas at Austin and doctorate degree in biomedical sciences from the University of Texas Graduate School of Biomedical Sciences, UT Health Science Center at Houston. She is a licensed pharmacist in Texas and a former NASA administrator's fellow.

A native of Ft. Worth, Texas, Dr. Milton is the wife of Michael Milton and the proud mother of two sons, Jonathan and Adrian.

Shirlette Glover Milton, Ph.D., R.Ph.

Assistant Dean
Student Services & Associate Professor
College of Pharmacy and Health Sciences
Texas Southern University

D r. Felecia M. Nave is the associate provost & associate vice president for academic affairs at Prairie View A&M University. She also serves as an associate professor of chemical engineering in the Roy G. Perry College of Engineering.

As an academic officer of the university, she is involved with curriculum reviews, enrollment management, on-going effectiveness initiatives and general student success. In addition to her academic affairs duties, Nave's research interests include: functionalized membranes, bioseparations, transport in cardiovascular system, women issues in engineering, K-12 outreach, gifted and talented African Americans pursuing STEM careers, and engineering education.

Nave received her undergraduate degree in chemistry from Alcorn State University and master's and doctorate degrees in chemical engineering from the University of Toledo. She is the recipient of numerous awards and honors including the 2008 Prairie View A&M University College of Engineering Service Award, Carl Storm Underrepresented Minority Fellowship - Gordon Conference, Texas A&M University Michael E. DeBakey Institute Fellow, Office of Naval Research (ONR) Historically Black Engineering College Future Faculty Fellowship.

Dr. Felecia M. Nave

Associate Provost & Associate Vice President
Academic Affairs
Prairie View A&M University

Aiesha Odutayo

Educator/Author
Houston I.S.D

Aiesha Odutayo is a science teacher for Houston I.S.D. In this position, she helps implement quality programs that foster children's academic and leadership skills. She was the recipient of the Young Outstanding Educator and Outstanding Climate Award.

Aiesha is the Author of *Science is the Key to Unlocking your Dreams, Odutayo's Test Taking Strategies,* and *The Wonderful World of Science.* Her books were written to help students develop an interest for science and develop effective strategies when taking science tests.

Aiesha is a member of the NAACP, where she serves as an executive committee member. She is also a member of Top Ladies of Distinction. She is also a member of the Houston Teacher Zoo Council where she serves as a facilitator to help the Houston Zoo's education department provide quality programs. Aiesha is a mentor for The Houston Police Department's YPAC Program.

Aiesha received a bachelor of social sciences degree from the University of Houston- Downtown.

Aiesha enjoys traveling and has visited over 30 countries.

Dr. Lillian B. Poats

Professor, Department of Educational Administration & Foundations
Texas Southern University

Dr. Lillian B. Poats is a professor in the department of educational administration and foundations at Texas Southern University, and director of certification for the College of Education. She earned a bachelor's degree in secondary education from Purdue University, and a master's degree in counseling and a doctor's degree in higher education administration from Texas Southern University.

Poats has numerous professional presentations and publications. Her publications include "Achieving Cultural Diversity: Meeting the Challenge" in *Diversity, Disunity and Campus Community*; "Challenges for Women of Color in Historically Black Colleges and Universities" in *Women As School Executives: Voices and Visions*; and "Working Collaboratively: Strategies for Success" in *Student Retention-Success Models In Higher Education.* Other publications include "Cultural and Ethnic Diversity in Texas Schools: Implications for Leadership Effectiveness" in *Texas Public School Organization and Administration*; and "Building a Village: The Impact of Connections on the Academic Success of Black Males" in *HBCUs Models of Success: Supporting Achievement and Retention of Black Males.*

She is married to Greyling Byron Poats, and they have one adult son, Greyling Byron Poats II.

Sheleah D. Reed, executive director of public relations for Prairie View A&M University, works to promote of the University to all of its stakeholders. This is done by developing marketing materials, press releases, advertising and other initiatives that communicate the student, faculty, alumni and research achievements.

For more than a decade, she has worked in the field of communications focusing on branding, crisis communications and marketing including stints at The Princeton Review and Texas Southern University. Additionally, she promoted the importance of membership banking for Security One Federal Credit Union and PrimeWay Federal Credit.

Her scope of duties recently increased to include the management of alumni relations, utilizing her skills to increase engagement and strengthen the bonds between the university and its graduates. In the past year, she has supervised the creation of "Down That Road: A Pictorial History of Prairie View A&M University" and 1876, the university's new magazine.

A Houston native, Reed earned a bachelor's degree in communications from Prairie View A&M University, followed by a master's degree in journalism and public relations from TCU. She plans to pursue a doctorate degree in mass communications.

Sheleah D. Reed
Executive Director of Communications
Prairie View A&M University

As president of Bay Ridge College, Dr. Stanford Simmons is in the process of transforming a 58-year-old, four-year Bible college into a residential junior college for African-American males, ages 18 to 21. The college is located in Kendleton, Texas, just south of Richmond-Rosenberg, off Highway 59. The college is scheduled to re-open in the fall of 2012.

Simmons has held community college administrative positions at Yosemite Community College; American River Community College; City Colleges of Chicago and Harper College. He also worked in corporate America as a Community Relations and Marketing Representative for Pacific Gas and Electric Company.

Simmons earned a Doctor of Education degree in higher education organization and leadership from the University of San Francisco. He also earned a master's degree in organizational communication from the University of the Pacific in Stockton, California, and a bachelor's degree in psychology from Northern Illinois University in DeKalb, Illinois.

Dr. Simmons and his wife Beverly have three children and seven grandchildren. He is a member of Triumph Champion Center in Richmond and a member of the Alpha Eta Lambda Chapter of Alpha Phi Alpha Fraternity, Inc.

Dr. Stanford Simmons Sr.
President & Chairman of the Board
Bay Ridge College

Emma Joahanne Thomas-Smith, Ph.D.

Provost and Senior Vice President
for Academic Affairs
Prairie View A&M University

Dr. Emma Joahanne Thomas-Smith is the provost and senior vice president for academic affairs at Prairie View A&M University. Known throughout the U.S. as a scholar and educator, she has been featured in numerous publications, National Public Radio (NPR) and the Fox Television Network.

Her professional appointments include the Certification Advisory Council of the Texas Higher Education Coordinating Board (THECB), secretary of the editorial board of the Negro Educational Review and the Computer-Assisted Composition Journal, the American Association of State Colleges and Universities (AASCU) and the National Association of State Universities and Land Grant Colleges (NASULGC).

She earned a bachelor's degree from Tuskegee University, a master's degree from New Mexico Highlands University and a doctoral degree from Washington State University. Her post-doctoral work includes studies at Northeastern University and the University of Texas at Arlington.

Her many honors, awards and memberships include Sigma Tau Delta International Honor Society, Phi Delta Kappa Education Honor Society, distinguishable alumnae at New Mexico Highlands University, Circle Award Winner, Zeta Phi Beta Sorority, Inc., Clear Lake Chapter and the Houston Chapter of the Links, Inc.

Willie F. Trotty, Ph. D.

Vice President for Research
Dean, Graduate School
Prairie View A&M University

Willie F. Trotty is the vice president for research, dean of the graduate school and professor of educational leadership at Prairie View A&M University. At the state and national levels, Trotty co-chairs the advisory committee for the Texas Leadership Institute (TLI), is a member of the board of directors of the Texas Society for Biomedical Research, chair of the Steering Committee for the Science and Engineering Alliance (SEA) in Washington, D.C., and Councilor and a Trustee of the Texas A&M Research Foundation. He is a past president of the Association of Texas Graduate Schools (ATGS) and the Council of Historically Black Graduate Schools (CHBGS). In December 2004, Trotty was a Fulbright Scholar at Ain Shams University in Cairo, Egypt.

Trotty received bachelor's degrees in biology and political science and master's degrees in biology and secondary education from Stephen F. Austin State University. He received a doctorate degree in educational administration and industrial management from Purdue University. In 1995, he completed the Governor's Executive Development Program (Class XIII) at the University of Texas Lyndon B. Johnson School Of Public Affairs in Austin, Texas.

N e'Cauje Turner began her career in the classroom and now has worked in the education field in many capacities. She currently works for the Cooperative for After-School Enrichment (CASE), which is a division of the Harris County Department of Education in Houston, TX. There she writes curriculum for after-school programs, manages program budgets and builds relationships with community stakeholders. An educator at heart, Ne'Cauje continues to cultivate minds as an adjunct professor at Houston Community College.

Ne'Cauje holds board positions at the Scleroderma Foundation, Texas Bluebonnet Chapter and the Hanover Homeowners Association. She is also a member of the National Urban League Young Professionals and a mentor.

Ne'Cauje received a Bachelor of Arts degree in political science from Southern University and A&M College in Baton Rouge, Louisiana, and a Master of Arts degree in public administration from Texas Southern University in Houston.

She is also a vegan, who enjoys running half-marathons.

Ne'Cauje Turner

CASE Models Coordinator
Harris County Department of Education

F red Washington is the vice president for administrative and auxiliary services and athletic director at Prairie View A&M University. From football to facilities, Washington's time and efforts are dedicated to ensuring students function in an environment conducive to learning.

Washington is responsible for all the support services at the school including housing, public safety and other aspects that affect the quality of life at the university. He manages the athletic program, which has seen particular success in the past few years, namely the SWAC Championship in football and championships in women's basketball. Under his leadership, PVAMU has a 66 percent graduation rate among student athletes, second only to Rice University in the state of Texas.

Washington also serves as a Major in the United States Army Reserve and is in his 21st year of service in that regard. He is currently serving as a senior trainer for the 75th Division in Houston.

Washington has earned two degrees from Prairie View A&M University: Bachelor of Business Administration in Accounting in 1992 and Master of Business Administration in Management in 1996.

Fred Washington

Vice President
Administrative and Auxiliary Services & Athletic
Director
Prairie View A&M University

Dr. James A. Wilson, Jr.

Director of the Honors Program
Associate Provost of Academic Affairs
Prairie View A&M University

Dr. James A. Wilson, Jr. is the director of the honors program and associate provost of academic affairs at Prairie View A&M University. He has previously served as professor in the history department at the University of Texas at Austin.

Wilson was a research fellow at Oxford and Cambridge Universities in England and the University of Nairobi in Kenya. He received the "Outstanding Young Texas Exes Award," from the alumni association at the University of Texas in 2004. For over 25 years, Wilson has traveled extensively throughout Africa. His love for the study of African history and culture began during his three-year tour with the U.S. Peace Corps in Kenya.

Wilson received his undergraduate degree in political science and English from the University of Texas in Austin in 1984. He earned a doctorate degree in history from Princeton University in 2002 and immediately began his academic career at Wake Forest University in Winston-Salem, North Carolina. Wilson holds a master of arts degree in history from Princeton University, a master's degree in African and African-American history from Cornell University and a certificate in African languages from the University of Florida.

Dr. George C. Wright

President
Prairie View A&M University

Dr. George C. Wright is the seventh president of Prairie View A&M University, a 135-year old HBCU.

Prior to joining the PVAMU family, Wright was executive vice-president for academic affairs and provost at the University of Texas at Arlington. Prior to assuming that post, he was provost and vice president for academic affairs. In 1993, he joined the faculty at Duke University as vice provost for university programs and director of the Afro-American studies program. He also held the William R. Kenan, Jr., Chair in American History. He served as an assistant professor, associate professor, professor and was the holder of the Mastin Gentry White Professorship of Southern History, and vice provost for undergraduate education at the University of Texas at Austin.

Wright is a noted African-American scholar, author and has been the recipient of numerous fellowships, grants and awards.

A native of Lexington, Kentucky, Wright received his bachelor and Master of Arts degrees in history from the University of Kentucky and his doctorate in history from Duke University. In 2004, Dr. Wright was awarded an honorary doctorate of Letters from the University of Kentucky.

Houston's
ENTREPRENEURS

EXPLORER

INDUSTRIALIST

PIONEER

CAPITALIST

TYCOON

HEROIC

PHILANTHROPIC

HUMANITARIAN

TRAILBLAZER

Doris Martin Barrow, III

President and Founder
Makeda Group & Associates

Joi Beasley

President & Chief Executive Officer
GOGO Business Communications Inc.

Doris Martin Barrow, III, MBA, is president and founder of Makeda Group & Associates, a sales growth and business development organization. In this role, he leads a team that provides strategic business consulting supported by a portfolio of customized and scalable solutions. Makeda Group guides its clientele to a performance-driven culture and a distinct competitive advantage within their industry, resulting in measurable improvements in top-line sales and bottom-line profitability.

Prior to founding Makeda Group, Doris held several positions, which served to hone his business acumen as an expert within the field of customer-focused selling.

He received his bachelor of arts degree from Grambling State University in 1998 and was awarded a master of business administration degree from Webster University in 2003.

He is a faithful servant of St. Monica Catholic Church in Houston, Texas and is a native of Opelousas, Louisiana.

Joi Beasley is the president and chief executive officer of GOGO Business Communications Inc. GOGO is a Houston based business-to-business expert in marketing, print-on-demand and graphic design. Beasley has more than a 15-year history in the document management industry. She is experienced in executive management, training, organizational development, human resources and operations.

GOGO is an Emerging 10 Award winner of the Houston Minority Supplier Diversity Council. Listed as one of the "Top 25 Women of Houston" by *Rolling Out* magazine in 2010, Beasley is a member of the Houston Citizen's Chamber of Commerce, Women's Business Enterprise Alliance and Delta Sigma Theta Sorority, Inc. She respectfully serves on the board of directors for Alzheimer's Association's Houston and Southeast Chapter and the Houston Downtown Alliance.

Prior to GOGO, Beasley ended her corporate career as the vice president of human resources for OnSite Sourcing in Alexandria, Virginia. Preceeding years were spent with IKON Office Solutions as director of employee relations and director of diversity. A native of Omaha, Nebraska, she is a proud Fisk University Alum and completed her graduate studies in industrial/ organizational psychology at University of Tulsa.

Jeffrey L. Boney

Founder and Chief Executive Officer
Texas Business Alliance

Tasha Bowen

Founder & Chief Executive Officer
Lofton Urban Development

Jeffrey L. Boney is the founder and chief executive officer of the Texas Business Alliance, a nonprofit organization with a mission to equip minority and women-owned businesses to be qualified suppliers, ready to compete for public, private and international opportunities. Jeffrey focuses on the unique needs of small businesses, helping them to operate and grow more efficiently through education, financing and business development strategies.

Jeffrey is president and chief executive officer of BoneFide Development and Investment Group, the parent company of Tax Service Express, BoneFide Accounting, BoneFide Realty and BoneFide Consulting. He is an adjunct professor in the school of Business Administration at Houston Community College.

Staying connected to the community, Jeffrey serves in the following capacities: member of the 100 Black Men of America, advisory board member for the Small Business Administration and the Port of Houston Authority.

Jeffrey earned a bachelor's degree in business management and finance from Texas Southern University, and is a member of Leadership Houston Class XXVII.

A native Houstonian, Jeffrey is married to Sharwin and has three beautiful children, Sariah, Jasmine, and Joshua.

Tasha Bowen currently serves as the president of the Women's Council of the Houston Real Estate Association. A real estate expert for more than seven years, she previously served as senior sales executive for Beltway Realty, assisting first time homebuyers and managing government and bank owned properties. Tasha currently owns and operates Lofton Urban Development, a commercial real estate development and consulting firm that assists faith-based organizations in their community development and growth needs.

In this position she helps organizations to acquire funding, build community centers, renovate or purchase new facilities and land acquisitions. She also prepares ministries to own and operate income producing divisions such as senior living facilities and multifamily housing units. Her nonprofit agency P.U.S.H. continues to give back to the community by teaching homeownership and financial literacy classes.

Tasha has received a host of awards and appeared on various media outlets such as *Channel 11 with Debra Duncan, Daystar Television Network* and *Impact Houston 100.7 FM.* Her hobbies include participating in church activities, dance choreography and spending time with her daughter.

Dwight Boykins

President/CEO
d Boykins Consulting Firm

Jeri Brooks

Lead Strategist & Principal
One World Strategy Group

Dwight Boykins is President/CEO of d Boykins Consulting Firm with offices in Houston and Washington, D.C.

He is a member at Windsor Village United Methodist Church and is involved in several community projects.

During the aftermath of Hurricane Ike, Dwight was asked by then Mayor, Bill White, to serve on a special formed committee to distribute over $150 million to needy families in Houston and the surrounding areas.

He is in love with his wife of 22 years and enjoys family and friends.

Jeri J. Brooks serves as lead strategist and principal for One World Strategy Group (One World). One World is a Houston-based strategic communications firm, founded in 2004, that offers internal and external communications services to our clients. Rooted in the performance improvement process they create communications strategies to develop your brand, your people and your process. From training programs and executive coaching to creative marketing ideas, One World delivers strong project management and overall strategic direction every time.

Over the past 15 years, Jeri has successfully built company brands, developed organizational culture and led community engagement projects. Brooks is responsible for a 60% increase in the client penetration of local nonprofit Legacy Community Health Services, the development of an eight-part customer service video training program for Houston Police Federal Credit Union and electing Mayor Annise Parker in the 2009 race.

She holds a bachelor of arts degree in communications, specializing in public relations and advertising from Southern Illinois University and a master of arts with a focus in organizational meaning systems from the University of Illinois.

Veronica Bush

Owner,
VBMedia Group

Gregory Cleare

Owner
Cleare Financial Services

Since 1993, Veronica has engaged as a consultant for image branding and strategic marketing for an international tourism board, well known corporate and business leaders, distinguished organizations, and prominent pastors across the nation.

In recognition of professional distinction and to further acknowledge personal and academic achievements, Veronica has reached a level of recognizable success in her respective field.

Veronica has expanded her service to entrepreneurs by placing small business owners and organizations on the fast track to success involving solid structuring, financing, and colossal target marketing. She is the founder of NuAchievers Correlation Community, a Social Network where members are given a platform for global exposure and empowered to achieve their goals and more.

Veronica is a leader, motivator, mentor and trendsetter in the faith-based community, small business sector and beyond. Veronica is contracted as a mastermind marketing consultant motivational speaker, seminar and workshop presenter, peer coach, media strategist, publicist, voiceover talent, virtual assistant or webmaster.

Gregory Cleare is the owner and senior financial advisor with Cleare Financial Services, which specializes in investments and financial planning for today's busy professional. Gregory also owns and operates Trace Pharmacy, a boutique pharmacy that is committed to superior service and the rebuilding of patient-pharmacist relationships to further promote overall patient health. This spring, Gregory plans to open his second pharmacy location in Sugar Land, Texas.

A native of Miami, Florida, Gregory's volunteer experiences include working with students at Texas Southern University College of Pharmacy and Health Sciences, the Houston Food Bank and Interfaith Ministries. His past and current memberships include the Houston Area Urban League Young Professionals, the NAACP and the Texas Southern University Alumni Association.

Gregory holds a bachelor's degree from Texas Southern University. He is a proud husband and father of three and enjoys weight training, traveling and spending time with family and friends.

Dannette Kay Davis

Principal
Kay Davis Associates, LLC

Jan A. Davis

Founder & President
SuperbTech Inc.

Dannette Davis has served as principal of Kay Davis Associates for 11 years where she oversees her company's day-to-day operations, which include outsourced construction project management, move management as well as contract Furniture, Fixtures and Equipment (FFE) sales and consulting.

Dannette has more than 28 years of experience in the construction industry specializing in facility planning, space planning and project management.

She is also founder and CEO of Insight Production Company, a unique corporate training and performance arts troupe.

Dannette serves on the boards of Houston Citizen Chamber of Commerce and Angelles Project. She is an active member of the Houston Minority Supplier Development Council and International Facility Management Association. She is also artistic director for Kingdom Players, a theatre ministry of Windsor Village United Methodist Church.

Dannette holds a bachelor of telecommunications from Texas Southern University and has completed masters work in construction management from the University of Houston.

Dannette is married to Edwin H. Davis and together they have three (3) children, Chelsea M. McElroy-Jenkins, Mitchell R. McElroy and Forrest H. Davis.

Jan A. Davis is founder and president of SuperbTech Inc., a 13 year old staffing firm specializing in staffing services for refinery, utility, governmental, industrial and commercial clients. Contract staffing services are performed in Texas, California, South Carolina, and Nevada, while permanent placement staffing services are performed nationwide.

Both Jan and her company are committed to community work. She is an active board member serving on the Special Needs Network nonprofit board, providing support and advocacy to underserved families with autistic children. She also serves as a finance committee board member to St. Brigid Catholic Church.

SuperbTech has committed to making an annual donation to the Playa Sunrise Rotary Teacher's Mini Grant Program. This program provides grants for Special Projects, Science Fairs, Trips, etc. to public and private elementary, middle, and high schools in the local LAX area.

Davis is a graduate of California State University, Northridge, with a bachelor of arts in sociology.

Her life passions include her 16-year-old son, Mark, international travel and maintaining a balanced well rounded life.

Derek Deyon, Esq.

Founder
The Deyon Law Group, P.L.L.C.

Niles Dillard

Chief Executive Officer & Executive Producer
Superior Video Productions Inc.

Derek Deyon is the founding attorney of the Deyon Law Group, P.L.L.C. In this capacity, Derek handles all aspects of entertainment law including entertainment transactions and litigation. To date, Derek has negotiated music production and publishing agreements between clients such as Lloyd Banks of G-Unit Records, Day 26 of Bad Boy Records, Jacob Latimore of Jive Records, and Teddy Riley. Derek also advised George Clinton on how to reclaim his music publishing catalogue and assisted George with ending fraudulent copyright filings at the U.S. Copyright Office

Derek earned a B.M. in music business & management from the Berklee College of Music in 2003, and a J.D., *cum laude* from the Thurgood Marshall School of Law in 2010. As a law student, Derek served as senior editor of the *Thurgood Marshall Law Review,* won first place in the Black Entertainment & Sports Lawyers Association's sixth annual scholarship Legal Writing Competition, and earned a CALI Excellence for the Future award in sports law. Derek is a member of the Texas State Bar and Alpha Phi Alpha Fraternity, Inc., among other organizations.

Niles Dillard is the chief executive officer and executive producer of Superior Video Productions, Inc. As founder and owner, he is a recognized leader in producing visual media solutions including filming, editing and producing corporate, commercial and event productions.

Niles has over 15 years of production experience. His client base includes: Deloitte, Double Tree/Hilton Hotel Companies, Prairie View A&M, Extreme Makeover Home Edition and Houston Independent School District. Niles was awarded a contract with the NFL SuperBowl XXXVIII and the 2011 NCAA Final Four.

A native Houstonian and graduate of Prairie View A & M University, Niles earned his bachelor's degree in accounting. He is an active volunteer in the community, and has volunteered for College Bound Technology Entrepreneurs, TTOI Summer Internship Program, and a Career Day presenter for local middle and high schools in the Houston area.

Niles Dillard has appeared in *Who's Who in Black Houston,* area weddings, *Wedding Pages Magazine, Jet Magazine* and was featured on *Channel 13* and in the *Houston Chronicle.*

Niles is married to Deandrea Dillard and the proud father of their two kids, Norris and Lauren.

James J. Donatto

Owner
Academy Awards

Veronica D. Frazier

President
Authentic Technology Solutions

James J. Donatto, II is a native Houstonian who holds a BBA from Texas Southern University with a focus in marketing. He has previously held positions in the Mayor's Office for the City of Houston, and as an Insurance Agent with both Farmer's and State Farm Insurance. Today, Mr. Donatto plays an intricate role in his family owned business, Academy Awards, an awards, apparel, and marketing products company, which after 23 years has become a staple in the business community. James also assist clients with their corporate and/ or personal branding through another family owned business 20.10 Media. His most recent business venture is MyCampaignStaff.com. MyCampaignStaff.com is a full service marketing and consulting firm that offers services and products ranging promotional items and signage to political and marketing strategies, consulting, and implementation. Whether, a full scale marketing or political campaign they pride themselves in being "Your One Stop Campaign Shop".

James Donatto, II is a member of the National Area Urban League Young Professionals, NAACP, Greater Houston Partnership, National Black MBA Association, and a founding member of the Momentum PAC.

Veronica D. Frazier is the president of Authentic Technology Solutions, a woman owned small business that provides information technology consulting to the public and private sector. Veronica has an extensive knowledge of technical support that optimizes business operations and enhancements for critical decisions making. Authentic Technology Solutions provides a broad range of unique solutions that uncover inefficiencies through - project management and provide valuable decisions with relevant business intelligence.

She received a bachelor of science degree in 1993 and a master of science degree in 1996, both from Texas Southern University in computer science. She is also a certified minority supplier with the Houston Minority Supplier Development Council and associated with many other organizations.

A native of Houston, Texas, Veronica is the wife of Derwin K. Frazier and the proud mother of two sons, Isaiah and Allen.

Arthur L. Fuller

Owner
ArtFul Enterprises International

Lloyd Gite

Owner, Art Broker
The Gite Gallery

ArtFul Enterprises International is an e-commerce affiliate marketing personal franchising business providing individual access to independent business ownerships. Previously, Arthur was a supervisory naval architect, mathematician and computer development director for the Naval Ship Systems Command Computer Aided Ship Design and Construction Project in Washington, D.C.

A computer graphics pioneer, Arthur developed the first machine-independent interactive graphics program. He has served as chair of the American National Standards Institute Committee, which developed the computer graphics standard, and is a founding member and nationally elected board member of the National Computer Graphics Association. He is also executive secretary of the Houston Business & Professional Men's Club.

Arthur's achievements include three outstanding performance awards, numerous technical papers and presentations in the United States and Europe on CAD and graphics, and an Outstanding Community Service Commendation from the Washington, D.C. City Council.

He earned a bachelor's degree in mathematics from Miles College in Birmingham, Alabama, and was a graduate fellow of applied mathematics at the New York University Courant Institute of Mathematical Sciences.

Lloyd Gite is owner of The Gite Gallery, showcasing treasures of African-native artists. He travels to the continent regularly, hand selecting the art, knowing his purchases help improve the quality of life for the artists' families. Lloyd uses his keen eye for contemporary African art and its interior placement to decorate clients' homes or businesses with art from his gallery.

Lloyd's clients are comprised of first time buyers, well-established clients, and celebrities such as Beyonce', Tina Knowles and NFL players Vince Young, Mario Williams and Andre Johnson.

Lloyd's former career in journalism led him to travel extensively throughout Africa, Asia, Europe, the Middle East and the Caribbean. His work garnered many awards including a National Association of Black Journalists Award in the category of International Reporting for a five-part series on South Africa and the Houston Area Urban League's communicator of the year award. He has also been honored as the National Black MBA communicator of the year.

He received his bachelor's degree in political science and history from North Texas State University, and his master's degree in radio, television and film from the University of Michigan.

Corey Green

President
Mosaic Media Solutions/MartianPrint.com

Monica Hancock

Founder & Owner
Custom Creations by Monica

Corey Green is the president of Mosaic Media Solutions and its subsidiary, MartianPrint.com. In this capacity, Corey serves as one of the few African American owners of a combined CD/DVD and print manufacturing company. Mosaic, founded in 1995, has continually flourished in the years following his acquisition.

Corey is also very active in community services and in 2006, along with Corey Garrett and Martin Troupe, founded CCM Foundation/HIVawareness.org. CCM is a nonprofit organization that promotes awareness and prevention of HIV/STDs, focusing on black and minority youths. Corey and CCM have been instrumental in recruiting top entertainers from r&b, hip hop and gospel for their signature community events, such as Don't Sleep On It!, Swishahouse World AIDS Day, The Pimp C. Health/Wellness Festival and their continuing PSA campaign. Corey, in 2008, was honored with a Congressional Letter on Commendation from Congressman Al Green.

Corey attended Texas A&M University where he majored in computer science and is the custodial parent of his two teenaged daughters, Jasmine and Justine.

Monica Hancock is the founder and owner of Custom Creations by Monica. An interior decorating company which specializes in custom window fashions was launched in 1992. The company services residential and commercial clients in Houston and the surrounding areas. Her clientele includes numerous clients of Cantoni, a high end contemporary furniture store located in Houston and clients of local and national Interior Designers. As a window fashions certified professional, Monica prides herself on creating unique and innovative window fashions for each individual client.

Monica is an active member of The Church Without Walls and is actively involved in the Economic Empowerment Business Ministry and the Greeter's Ministry. She also had the opportunity to design custom window fashions for her pastor's office and suite.

Monica was an African American business achievement pinnacle award finalist in 2003 which was associated with the Houston Citizens Chamber of Commerce. Her professional memberships include the Interior Design Society, the Greater Houston Builders Association and the Window Fashions Certified Professionals.

A native of Houston, Texas, Monica completed studies in business administration from the University of Houston.

Arquella Hargrove

Human Resources Management
Settlement Facility Dow Corning Trust

LaQuinta Donatto Harris

Owner & Chief Executive Officer
Academy Advertising Specialties and Awards

Arquella Hargrove is a business-savvy human resources leader with a track record of developing and executing HR strategies that help grow the business operations. She implements best practices that positively enhances the bottom line and satisfies the client. Arquella's expertise includes strategic planning, compliance, employee relations, training, program development and general human resources administration.

Arquella is one of the founding members and the current Houston Chapter president for the National Association of African Americans in Human Resources. In addition to this role, Arquella heads the human resources department for the Settlement Facility Dow Corning Trust. She is an avid networker and involved with numerous organizations offering her expertise as a resource.

Arquella has completed an executive master's degree in business administration from Texas Woman's University. She is also certified as a business life coach, administering DISC and Birkman Behavioral Personality Assessments.

Arquella and her husband, Dexter Hargrove, reside in the Houston area and are the proud parents of Gabriel and Margaret.

At the tender age of 22 Mrs. Harris' highly developed entrepreneurial drive led her to become the owner and chief executive officer of her own industrial tag business. Harris' record breaking sales figures, garnered her recognition as "Entrepreneur of the Year" from many organizations.

Today, Harris spends much of her time managing *Academy Advertising Specialties and Awards,* a full service Awards Store, with 22 employees offering engraving, embroidery, and screen-printing in Midtown. Academy Awards produces over one million advertising specialty awards and wearable items annually.

Harris has gained a deeper appreciation of the values of hard work and instilled in her, at an early age by her parents, James and Mary Ann Donatto.

Harris is a native Houstonian and graduate of Duchesne Academy and Sweet Briar College in Virginia (BA) and LeTourneau University (MBA). Harris is an active member in many local community organizations and is married to Daniel Harris. They have two children, Layla and Langston. Harris enjoys spending time with friends and family, scuba diving and traveling the world.

Erinn Harrison Hartwell

Managing Partner
Erinn's Heart Early Learning Academy

Stephanie Hill-Polk

President
Quality Solutions Professional Services LLC

Erinn Harrison Hartwell is managing partner of Erinn's Heart Early Learning Academy located in historical mid-town Houston. In her position, she manages up to 10 full-time staff (teachers, aides and food nutritionists) as well as countless volunteers. Erinn serves on the board of the Shadow Creek Ranch Neighborhood Association, where she is board chair for The Carousel Kids Foundation, whose mission is to provide teacher curriculum training for upcoming child care centers in the Houston metropolitan area. She is founder and active participant of the 5K Run for Education, The Holiday Hopper Community Market, Balloons Galore, and a member of The Top Ladies of Distinction mentoring group.

Erinn's Heart was featured in the local Houston Community Paper (Midtown Paper).

Born and educated in Jackson, Mississippi. During school she was a cheerleader, candy striper at the local hospital and participated in the Cherry Blossom Parade in London, England. She later served as an Au Pair in Vienna, Austria and was a Miss Black Houston Pageant contestant.

Erinn is the wife of Rasheen Hartwell and the proud parent of one son, Tre' Christopher Hartwell.

Stephanie Hill-Polk is president of Quality Solutions Professional Services LLC (QSP), a full-service recruiting, staffing and consulting company located in Houston, Texas. Stephanie began QSP to assist those looking for the career of their dreams.

Stephanie was recognized by the Houston Minority Business Council for "teaming" with other minority owned organizations to provide quality solutions to her clients. Under her leadership, QSP has deployed a number of strategic initiatives to provide increasing levels of service to customers and employees. She quickly earned the trust of clients providing excellent service and reducing time-to-fill ratio.

Stephanie has more than 10 years experience working with small start-up organizations to Fortune 100 companies, in oil and gas technology and manufacturing industries. She has recruited for a variety of disciplines, including HR, HES, accounting/finance, geologists, reservoir engineers, facilities and design engineers, procurement, IT, assemblers, warehouse and administrative. Positions range from entry level to senior management level roles.

A native of Austin, Texas, Stephanie is married to Michael Polk, and is the mother of Virgal and Loren Hill, and stepmother to Michael, Adrian, Mia and Megan Polk.

Sharon C. Jenkins

Inspirational Principal
The Master Communicator & Associates

Cornell L. Johnson

President & CEO
CandCNET Associates Inc.

Sharon C. Jenkins is a motivational speaker, workshop facilitator and serves as the inspirational principal for The Master Communicator and Associates. She is the mastermind behind the successful 2011 Authors Networking Summit, which started its national tour in April 2011, as well as the tele-class facilitator for Powerful Women International.

Known as "The Master Communicator," Jenkins is proficient in communicating the plight of the abused child in her revelatory book, *Beyond the Closet Door*. In her advocacy she has also started a writer's workshop series for children called Speak Little Children Writer's Initiative.

Jenkins is an avid writer and has written for *Gospel Truth* magazine and newspaper, *Just* magazine, *Houston Style*, *D-Mars Faith-Based Journal* and is presently a contributor to *Beauty Come Forth*, an e-magazine. She has also co-authored two other books, *Songs of Three Sisters* and *Ready, Set, Succeed, Making Your Dream Come True*.

Jenkins, an MLK scholar, is currently working on a doctorate degree at Union Institute and University, with a concentration in public policy and social justice.

Cornell L. Johnson is president and chief executive officer of CandCNET Associates Inc., a premier IT system integrator. His primary responsibility is to carry out the strategic objectives of his company, including the logical development of products and services that bring value to the customers and the companies stakeholders. In December of 2010, CandCNET was awarded and recognized as an Emerging Ten Company by the Houston Minority Supplier Development Council and Halliburton.

As a practicing quality analyst, Cornell has recently received both the Lean Six Sigma, and the Lean Six Green Belt and is close to achieving the Lean Six Sigma Black Belt. The attainment and implementation of these tools has had an encouraging effect on the company's delivery of IT intrusion detection for security and fire alarm system and other products and services.

Cornell is an active member of several professional organizations and currently serves on board of directors of the Native American Chamber of Commerce and EcoGreen Energy Solutions.

In discussions he often quotes Booker T. Washington, who said "Excellence is to do a common thing in an uncommon way."

Magoe Johnson

President
Images by Magoe Inc.

Alton LaDay

Principal
Alton LaDay Media

Magoe Johnson is president of Images by Magoe Inc., and is Houston's first black certified image professional with the Association of Image Consultants International (AICI). Magoe empowers individuals to enhance their image for their personal and professional lives.

She has presented seminars and briefings to corporations, Fortune 500 companies, academia and numerous industry organizations around the world, empowering individuals to capture opportunities as they arise, by communicating professionalism and confidence through the way they look and the manner in which they present themselves.

Native Texan Alton LaDay is the principal of Alton LaDay Media an award winning public relations firm specializing in the promotion of luxury goods, brands and services.

In 2009 Alton expanded his professional reach to television making regular appearances on the popular lifestyle program Wild About Houston.

Among numerous charitable efforts Alton co-chaired Herman Park Conservancy's Dancing under the Stars – the Urban Green Gala in November 2008; the Art 4 Life Auction in January 2009 and 2010, the 5th Annual Spacetaker Gala SYNERGY in February 2009 and Alton will co-chair the Houston Center for Contemporary Craft's Martini Madness in September of 2011.

Alton has been active with the Museum of Fine Art Houston's African American Art Advisory Association (Five A,) American Society of Interior Designers Industry Partners (ASID-IP), Fashion Group International, HRC Federal Club, National Association of Black Journalist and the Public Relations Society of America.

Alton resides in Houston's Museum District.

Dr. Verdi Lethermon

Author & Speaker

Jared L. Lofton

President & Real Estate Broker
Lofton Realty/Love Moving Company

Verdi Rountree Lethermon, Ph.D., the author of *When God Speaks, People Who Hear Are Healed,* is nationally known for her dynamic public speaking and Bible teaching. Her message of hope, healing and empowerment crosses age, cultural, economic and gender barriers as she passionately seeks to bridge the chasm between psychology and spirituality.

Dr. Lethermon is a sought after speaker for numerous universities, churches, and community and business organizations. Whether one-on-one or standing before hundreds, she intimately and personally connects with her audience from a place of authenticity and vulnerability.

The author earned her Ph.D. in Clinical Psychology from Louisiana State University. She has 24 years of counseling experience in private, legal, medical, business and educational settings. She has worked in the field of law enforcement for 16 years and is currently the Director of the Psychological Services Division for the Houston Police Department. In addition to her work at HPD, she has been in part-time private practice for approximately 15 years.

Dr. Lethermon and Walter Lethermon are the proud parents of a daughter, son-in-law, and two teenage sons.

Jared Lofton is the founder and real estate broker of Lofton Realty based in Houston, Texas. Lofton Realty is a residential real estate sales firm that is committed to serving clients in Houston and surrounding areas since 2006. In 2010 Lofton was selected by the National Association of Realtors as one of the Top 30 Realtors under 30 in the country. In addition to Lofton Realty, he also owns Love Moving Company, which offers clients local moving services in residential, commercial and industrial moves.

Lofton is a graduate from Southern University, where he received a Bachelor of Science degree in finance and economics. He also has a Master of Business Administration degree from Texas Southern University. He is an actor/model with Pastorini Bosby and has worked on several TV commercials, movies and short films. Lofton is committed to giving back to the community through his annual back to school fundraiser and Christmas toy drive for homeless kids in Houston & New Orleans.

Queen Ester Martin, DrPH

Executive Director
Sisterhood of Faith in Action

Michael R. Northington

Chief Executive Officer
Sparkle Cleaning Services, LLC

Dr. Queen Martin is the executive director of Sisterhood of Faith in Action, a nonprofit organization, which she founded in 1994. In December 2003, she founded her second nonprofit organization, Ed's World Inc. in memory of her son. She serves as the board president of Ed's World, focusing on empowering youth and young adults.

In the Houston community, Martin works to ensure that tutorials and college prep sessions are available to high school students. She continues her reach to international projects through Ed's World by collaborating with leaders in Nsawam, Ghana, to help repair a school, sponsor soccer competitions and promote academic success. She also serves as the vice president of the Acres Homes Super Neighborhood Council.

Martin earned a doctorate degree from the University of Texas, School of Public Health. She is an assistant professor at Prairie View A&M University, also overseeing student interns and serving as a faculty sponsor of the Student Health Organization. She has earned a Certified Health Education Specialist (CHES) designation.

She has two daughters and one son (deceased) and six grandchildren.

Michael R. Northington is the sole proprietor of Sparkle Cleaning Services, LLC ("SCS"). Since 1979, he has worked diligently in providing some of the best commercial cleaning maintenance in South Texas. His commitment to quality, detail, and professionalism has made him a premiere independent cleaning contractor. Michael manages several employees and has managed more than forty employees. He has maintained several contracts with multi-million dollar companies. His company specializes is providing commercial cleaning services that cater to single story buildings as well as multilevel buildings including churches, daycare centers, schools, industrial complexes, apartment complexes, construction clean-up and other types of commercial buildings.

Michael earned a Bachelors of Business Administration degree from Texas Southern University. He worked in corporate America several years prior to starting his own business in 1979. He has been active in his church ministry for many years and served as a volunteer for the Fort Bend County Boys & Girls Club. He has also been a motivational speaker at Houston area schools on starting your own business. In the future, he intends to expand SCS throughout the state of Texas and become more involved in helping in the development of underprivileged youth.

Glenn Outerbridge

Founder, President & CEO
eyeMe, LLC

Michael G. Polk

Owner
Quality Environmental Service

Glenn Outerbridge is the founder, president and chief executive officer of eyeMe, LLC. eyeMe is the next-generation social networking media service that allows users to uniquely create and share their personal story and legacy using a variety of multimedia formats. This unique social network is relevant from the time a baby is born and extends beyond the grave to memorialize others. eyeMe helps individuals experience self expression, fun and significant connections.

eyeMe's vision is to make a positive impact in the world by focusing on the positive things of life and giving people internet tools and services to help them focus on these positive things, feel good and share it with the people that mean the most to them.

Glenn's experience includes chief executive officer of Cybersoft NA, a software solutions company and 25 years of experience in executive management, software systems/solutions, finance and consulting. He is a successful executive with extensive skills in general business operations, business development and start-up operations.

Glenn holds a Bachelor of Science degree in accounting with concentrated studies in MIS from New Hampshire College.

As a result of 25 years of experience in quality control, engineering and auditing, Michael G. Polk is the owner of Quality Environmental Service and partner of Quality Solutions Professional Services LLC, located in Houston, Texas. He has a diverse in-depth knowledge and understanding in areas of design, the manufacturing process and control techniques. He delivers a vast range of products in the manufacturing, the industrial and the oil and gas industries.

Michael provides consulting for developing quality and environmental systems to be incompliance with ISO 9001 and ISO 14001, respectively. He has developed systems within companies to improve efficiencies and eliminate non-value added activities. He has also developed and performed quality management systems, internal auditing and ISO 9001 training for companies.

Michael is a graduate of Texas Southern University, earning a Bachelor of Science degree in industrial technology and engineering. He is married to Stephanie Hill-Polk and father of four children, Michael, Adrian, Mia and Megan Polk and stepfather to Virgal and Loren Hill.

Joie Rasberry

Owner
Joie Rasberry & Associates LLC

Kenneth Robinson Jr.

President & CEO
Kenneth Robinson, A Professional Corporation

Joie Rasberry is a highly sought-after professional orator and Christian speaker, author, speech writer and entrepreneur. She is the speaker of choice for Fortune 500 companies, universities and colleges, organizations, businesses, foundations, conferences, churches and gala affairs.

She has two books to her credit, *From Jensen Drive to Pennsylvania Avenue* and *More Than Half a Century,* as well as an award-winning motivational CD.

Rasberry owns Joie Rasberry & Associates LLC, an executive communications company offering speech coaching, speech writing and speech training to corporate, nonprofit and community-based organizations.

In addition, she is executive director and founder of Rasberry's House of Hope Inc., a state-licensed, non profit 501(c)(3) organization, established as a place of hope and healing for adolescent girls shattered by abuse, abandonment and neglect.

Rasberry received her theatrical education from The High School for the Performing and Visual Arts. She attended Southwestern Christian College for biblical studies and Texas Southern University for communications.

Kenneth Robinson Jr. is the president and chief executive officer of Kenneth Robinson, A Professional Corporation. Kenneth has designed and managed a variety of projects including affordable public housing, restaurants, casinos, schools, religious sanctuaries and single and multi-family residences. Kenneth takes great pride in his ability to complete projects on schedule and within the allowed construction budget.

Kenneth prides himself on quality and efficiency, and his company is equipped with the latest computer aided design technologies including 3-D walk and fly-through programs, that allow clients to experience spatial relationships in the early stages of the design process.

Kenneth received a bachelor's degree in architecture from Southern University A&M College in Baton Rouge, Louisiana. He is active in the Houston community, and has served as the board secretary for the 100 Black Men of Metropolitan Houston Chapter for the past three years.

A native of New Orleans, Louisiana, Kenneth is the proud father of one daughter, Chandler-Elizabeth.

Kim Roxie

Creative Director
Lamik Beauty

Venus L. Ruben

Owner & Lead Event Coordinator
Events by XOXO

Kim Roxie is the beauty genius of Lamik Beauty and a Southwest Houston native. With diverse clients such as P.Diddy, Chrisette Michele, Kim Burrell, and hometown favorite Yolanda Adams, brand recognition for Lamik is more apparent that ever before. Rated as "the best spot to get eyelashes, eyebrow sculpting and make-up application" by The Houston Chronicle, Lamik Beauty 's stylish boutique can be found in River Oaks in her native Houston, Texas, downtown Atlanta, and Oakwood Center Mall in New Orleans..

She is a member of Cosmetic Executive Women, National Black MBA, Spirit of Business Award Honoree of 2009, Rolling Out's Top 25 Women of Houston, 2009 Trailblazer of the Year from the National Association of Women Business Owners, and 2009 recipient of D-Mars Women in It to Win It. She created the "Make-Up with a Purpose" project where she speaks and instructs students aspiring in the beauty industry.

Kim Roxie holds a Bachelor of Arts degree in Public Relations from Clark Atlanta University, resides in Houston, Texas with her fiancé and is the proud aunt of 5 nephews.

Venus L. Ruben is owner and lead event coordinator of Events by XOXO, a boutique meeting and event planning company that combines fresh and edgy ideas and outlooks to produce events that people talk about for years to come.

Venus' strong reputation grew organically through her ability to stay calm in any situation and the essential belief to respect, understand and listen to her clients.

A member of Windsor Village United Methodist Church, her volunteer experiences include working with the Ronald McDonald House Charities, the Y-Me Foundation, Special Olympics Texas and the Diabetes Association of Houston.

Venus' past and current memberships include the Houston Area Urban League Young Professionals, Kappa Psi Pharmaceutical Fraternity, Inc., the Tri-Beta National Biological Honor Society, NAACP and the Young Black Scholars Honors Society.

Venus holds a bachelor's of science degree from Grambling State University, and will be awarded a doctorate degree in pharmaceutical sciences from Texas Southern University in May of 2012.

Wendell P. Shepherd Sr.

Owner & Principal
The Shepherd Law Firm

Rikki V. Smith

Owner & Chief Executive Officer
Smithwood Medical Institute LLC

Wendell P. Shepherd, Sr. is the owner and principal of The Shepherd Law Firm, a general civil litigation law firm in Sugar Land, Texas. Wendell manages a wide range of litigation, with a particular emphasis on construction property damage, commercial litigation, and business litigation.

Wendell graduated from The University of Texas at Austin with bachelor's degrees in Economics and History; a Master of Business Administration degree with concentrations in Finance and Management from The University of Houston, and a juris doctorate degree from South Texas College of Law

Wendell is a life member of The University of Texas at Austin Ex-Students Association and of Kappa Alpha Psi Fraternity, Inc. He is also a member of Windsor Village United Methodist Church and vice-president of the Board of Directors of the Sienna Plantation Youth Baseball League. In his spare time, Wendell enjoys traveling with his family; attending college and professional sporting events; and, managing his son's youth baseball teams.

A native of Carthage, Texas, Wendell is the husband of Barbara Shepherd and the proud father of Wendell P. Shepherd, Jr.

Rikki V. Smith is the owner and chief executive officer of Smithwood Medical Institute, LLC a company that provides certifications and training for healthcare careers. As a native of Bay City, Texas, Rikki is a graduate of The University of Texas at Austin where she achieved her Bachelor of Science in Advertising while double minoring in Corporate Communications and Business from the Red McCombs School of Business. She is currently attaining her MBA from St. Thomas University.

Rikki plays an active role within Alpha Kappa Alpha Sorority, Inc, Houston Area Urban League Young Professionals, Texas Exes, Andrew Smith Jr. Foundation, Momentum Pac, and Lakewood Church. Her passion and commitment for policy, politics, and being a part of the movement has been evident as she has participated in helping MPAC actively engage our peers on what is happening in our city's government.

Terry Smith

Founder & President
Smith & Company Architects

Lisa Williams Stillwell

Founder/Executive Director
Celebrating You LLC

Terry Smith is founder and president of Smith & Company Architects, a 10 person architectural firm based in Houston and founded in 1999. Terry's office is best known as the designer of the multi-award winning African American Library at the Gregory School in Houston's 4th Ward.

Smith participated in the design of some of Houston's most notable buildings including the Harris County Criminal Justice Center, the Houston Texans YMCA, and the proposed Sports Complex and Football Stadium at Prairie View A&M University. He designed facilities on other college campuses including Rice University, University of Houston, and Texas A&M University.

Terry's firm was awarded a 2010 Design Honor Award by the Houston chapter of the American Institute of Architects, and has also received design awards from the Greater Houston Preservation Alliance and the National Organization of Minority Architects. He is a 2008 Houston Minority Business Council Emerging 10 Award winner and in 2007 was listed in the *Houston Business Journal* as one of Houston's top minority owned business.

Lisa Williams Stillwell is founder and executive director of Celebrating You, a youth enrichment program dedicated to promoting leadership, character building, entrepreneurship, and employment skills. This program addresses issues and challenges of at risk and economically disadvantaged youth. Lisa, a presenter, facilitator, and speaker, is also a secondary educator in the Houston area. Lisa has a passion for young people and a strong desire for them to be productive and successful.

She has received numerous awards and honors including the Top 25 Women of Houston award by Rolling Out and Comerica Bank, Outstanding Teacher of the Year by the Houston Alliance of Black School Educators, Wal-Mart Teacher of the Year, Incredible Teacher of the Year by People's Trust Credit Union, and Master Certified Entrepreneurship Teacher of the Year by the National Foundation for Teaching Entrepreneurship of New York.

A native of Grambling, Louisiana, Lisa has a bachelor's degree in psychology from Grambling State University and a master's degree in public administration from the University of Washington.

Lisa and her husband, Samuel, have three children, Matthew, Brandon, and Samantha.

Dr. Anthony Taylor Sr.

Publisher, President & Chief Executive Officer
Business Pros Newspaper

Tracy Taylor-Smith

President & Chief Executive Officer
Taylor Smith Consulting, LLC

Dr. Anthony Taylor Sr. is president and chief executive officer of *Business Pros* newspaper and businesspros4u.com. Taylor is a publisher and a broker at Anthony Taylor Realty and has been described as the "complement package" to his involved endeavors and a jack-of-all-trades.

Knowledge and commitment epitomize his admired and valued business, education, law enforcement, philosophy, political, psychology, public speaking and theology experiences. He is the author of *Just Tell the Truth, Make It Happen: Traveling the Road of Life* and his best work, the new 2011 release, *You Made Me Love Your Man*.

Feeling that time spent in the community is more valuable than any amount of money, Taylor dedicates time to speak to kids, always appearing in person and never sending anyone to do his work. He cares for the community by initiating and completing many projects and is always working to make the community safer, whether he is providing jobs through his businesses, reporting poor building codes, or community safety issues.

Tracy Taylor-Smith is president & chief executive officer for Taylor Smith Consulting, LLC. As the owner of the firm, she directs all operational and contract services for the company. With offices located in Austin, Dallas, and Houston, Texas, Taylor Smith Consulting is a full service staffing, training and development, and management consulting firm that is committed to helping emerging and established companies gain greater operational efficiencies and increased customer and public satisfaction levels.

Tracy, a 2009 Houston Minority Supplier Development Council E-10 Award Winner and a 2008 Pinnacle Award Finalist, also serves as a member of the Advisory Board for the Texas Business Alliance.

With a background of over 20 years of experience in public administration, transportation, customer service, contract services, and management; Tracy holds degrees in Computer Science Technology, Business Management, and a certificate in Project Management.

A native of Houston, Texas, Tracy is the wife of William Smith and the proud mother of Chadrick, Nicholas, and Taylor.

Rick Wheeler

Owner & Chief Executive Officer
Wheeler Enterprises

Christopher Williams

Co-Founder
Ideas Unlimited LLC

Rick Wheeler is the owner and chief executive officer of Wheeler Enterprises, a mobile disc jockey service. He provides appropriate music to the appropriate event from numerous large companies attended by hundreds to small private settings, and occasionally travels hundreds of miles to provide his expertise.

Rick was a National Merit Scholarship recipient and attended Grambling State University, where he graduated, with honors, with a Bachelor of Arts degree in math and computer science. He previously worked for TEXACO where he was a senior information systems analyst, and for AT&T where he was a senior implementation manager and presently with IBM where he is an operations production analyst. In addition, he is a licensed real estate agent, loan officer and notary public in the state of Texas.

Rick, who is single, is originally from Shreveport, Louisiana, and is a proud member of Kappa Alpha Psi Fraternity, Inc. He is one of the founders and charter members of the Douglas L. Williams Alumni Chapter of Grambling State University and serves on the board of the Briargate Townhouse Homeowners Association, Inc.

Christopher Williams is the co-founder and managing partner of Ideas Unlimited LLC, which specializes in event marketing and event promotions. Williams is also co-founder of the Soulcial Series group, which was created to bring award winning and international performers from across the world, infused with local talent to Houston. The series not only includes the greatest artists from all over, but your local disc jockey that mixes that old and new school music to charm the soul.

A native of Beaumont, Texas, his volunteer experiences include working with students at the Youth Development Center, the United Negro College Fund and Order Steps. His past and current memberships include Alpha Phi Alpha Fraternity, Inc., Kappa Kappa Psi National Honorary Band Society and the Tri County Chamber of Commerce.

Williams holds a Bachelor of Science degree from Prairie View A&M University and a Master of Business Administration degree from the University of Phoenix. He is a proud father of a teenage daughter, Tamiah. When he is not working he enjoys golf, traveling and spending time with family and friends.

Margo E. Williams

President and Chief Executive Officer
MWH Public Relations

Kenneth Yellowe

Chairman & Chief Executive Officer
Global Energy Group

Margo E. Williams is president and Chief Executive Officer of MWH Public Relations, ranked by the Houston Business Journal as one of the top 25 public relations firms in Houston and 2010 American Marketing Association Marketer of the Year Award nominee. The firm is a full service public relations firm that creates memorable and enduring strategic campaigns for its clients. Through public and media relations, advertising, branding, graphic and Web design and event planning, MWH Public Relations provides value by assuring its clients' brand promise resonates with their customers so they successfully compete in the marketplace.

Margo is a Houston Achievement Place advisory board member; Leadership Houston Class XXI graduate; United Way Project Blueprint Class XXIII member, and a member of New Light Christian Center Church.

Margo has completed studies in English and business management from the University of St. Thomas and the University of Phoenix.

Originally from Chicago, Margo is the proud mother of Cederick Tardy II, an author, public speaker, prior U.S. Navy soldier and currently proudly serves the United States Army as a Second Lieutenant in the 36th Engineering Brigade in Fort Hood, Texas.

Chairman of Global Energy Group, Kenneth Yellowe is a successful and well-known U.S. based Nigerian entrepreneur and among the most dynamic businessmen currently operating on the African continent. Kenneth has founded several companies in the United States, Venezuela and Nigeria. He is an imaginative pioneer whose foresight and business acumen changed the Nigerian gas industry. His forte as the consummate dealmaker culminated in 1998 into the first indigenous gas processing company in Nigeria; Global Gas and Refining LTD.

Kenneth is an illustrious son of Bakana in the Degema Local Government Area of Rivers State, Nigeria. Starting from modest beginnings in Nigeria, he formed his first partnership as a teenager before sojourning to the United States for further studies.

Kenneth's network includes numerous heads of states and business leaders around the world. His humanitarian work is extensive with particular focus in healthcare and education for the underprivileged.

Kenneth loves God, humanity and family. He is married to Pamela and has five children.

Houston's COMMUNITY LEADERS

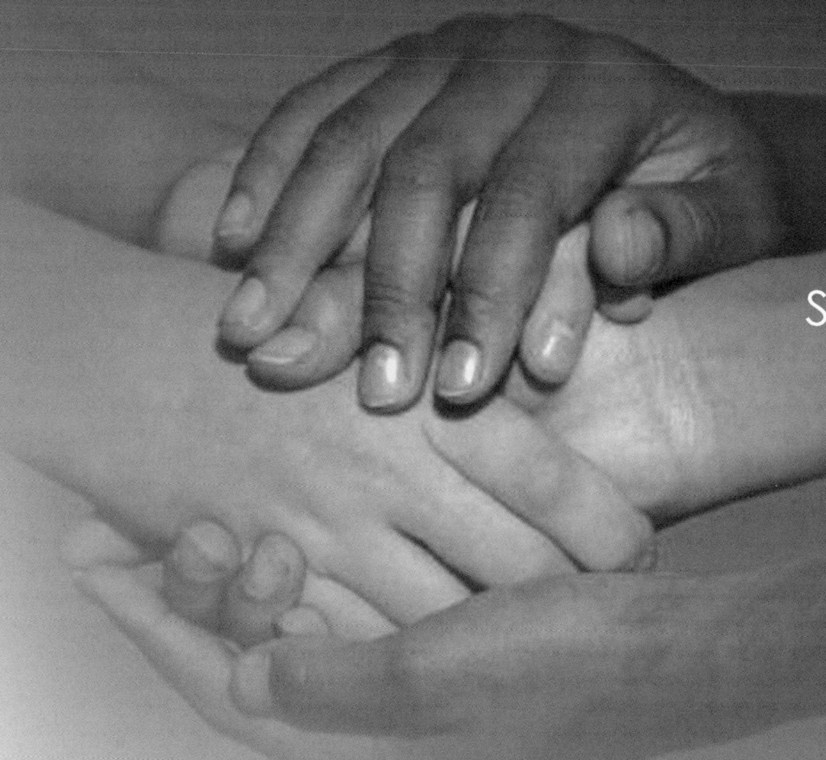

NOBLE

CARING

SELF-SACRIFICING

GENEROUS

EMPOWERING

HEROIC

PHILANTHROPIC

HUMANITARIAN

ALTRUISTIC

Dr. Leonard N. Barksdale

Pastor
Fifth Ward Missionary Baptist Church

Dr. Leonard Barksdale has served as pastor of Fifth Ward Missionary Baptist Church for 17 years and has been an attorney for 36 years. The church's 501(c)(3), Faith Revitalization Center Inc serves the Fifth Ward community.

Barksdale is past board chairman of the College of Biblical Studies and a board member of Habitat For Humanity. He serves on the Public Engagement Committee for the Houston Independent School District. He has lectured on law and religion to such institutions as the National Bar Association, the Thurgood Marshall School of Law, the Houston Graduate School of Theology, and the National Black Law Students Association.

Barksdale received a Bachelor of Arts degree from the University of Houston, a Master of Arts degree, summa cum laude, from the Houston Graduate School of Theology, a juris doctorate degree from the Texas Southern University School of Law, an Associate of Biblical Studies degree from the College of Biblical Studies and a graduate certificate from Dallas Theological Seminary.

He and his wife, Gladys, have been married for 36 years and have two daughters, Lea and Anita.

Jacqueline Whiting Bostic

Retired U.S. Postmaster
U.S. Postal Service

Jacqueline Whiting Bostic is a retired U.S. postmaster. Previously, she managed the mail delivery service, finances, employee facilities and community relations for a designated community.

Bostic received a Vounteer of the Year Award from the U.S. Postal Service, Southern Region. A member of Jack & Jill of America, Inc., she served as a local, regional and national officer. As president of the Houston Alumnae Chapter of Delta Sigma Theta Sorority, Inc., Bostic promoted social action. She served as president and chairman of the board of the Metropolitan Houston YWCA and was the first woman to serve as chairman of the board of the Houston Postal Credit Union. Bostic serves as a trustee for the YWCA Retirement Fund and treasurer of the Woman's Auxiliary of the National Baptist Convention USA. Additionally, she is president and chairman of Antioch Project Reach, Inc.

Bostic holds a Bachelor of Arts degree and attended Fisk University, Hofstra College and Texas Southern University. She is a widow, the proud mother of four and a grandmother.

Apostle Delores "D" Tyler Brown is founder of Inspirations of Hope® Global Ministries, which includes 4 Hope Unlimited Publishing, Split Water Records, B3 Marketing Group PR, Fresh Hope Bible Church, Texas Evangelism Alliance Ministries, King of Glory Prayer Network and Annual Texas "King of Glory" Leadership Prayer Summit.

She was blessed with apostolate commissioning by Apostle Vincent Pool. She was awarded a Bachelor of Business Administration degree from the University of Louisiana, Monroe, is a graduate from the Southwestern Paralegal Institute, attended South Houston Bible Institute and is a certified human behavior consultant.

Brown retired as a senior pensions analyst from Cooper Industries after 25 years. She is a contributing writer for the *Good News Monthly* newspaper, the *Prophet's Mantle* magazine and formerly for *Gospel Truth News-Houston*. She was awarded as one of the *Good News Monthly* Top 30 Men and Women of God in Southwest Texas in 2011. She is also an author and publisher.

A native of Bastrop, Louisiana, Brown is the wife of Lawrence Brown, has one son, Tracey, stepson, Michael and is the grandmother of Austin Devon Tyler.

Delores "D." Tyler Brown
Founder
Inspirations of Hope® Global Ministries

George E. Burrell Sr., is pastor of Internal Hope Fellowship Church, a church plant located in Friendswood, Texas. He formerly served 29 years as staff chaplain of Harris County Jail, in Houston, beginning as the first and only black staff chaplain in the history of the Harris County Jail.

Driven by a heartbeat to mentor teen boys and young adult men, in 2006, Burrell founded Young Men of Valor, an annual day of discussion, day of acceptance and day for change held at various churches throughout Houston.

A native of Beaumont, Texas, he attended University of Houston and holds bible certification from College of Biblical Studies. He is an alumnus of Billy Graham School of Evangelism and scholarship recipient of the E.K. Bailey International Conference on Expository Preaching. He's a member of Omega Psi Phi Fraternity, Inc., Omega Theta Chapter and past recipient of the Silver Award Recipient for community service from Harris County Council Organizations.

Burrell and the love of his life, Kathy, have three adult sons, two daughters-in-love and six grandchildren.

George E. Burrell Sr.
Pastor
Internal Hope Fellowship Church

Kathy A. Burrell

Executive Director & Founder
Earth's Angels Conference

Kathy A. Burrell is a native Houstonian. Kathy's life-long desire to disciple teen girls and young adult women, led her to birth a phenomenal conference for teen girls and young adult women, *Earth's Angels* Conference; 2012 will mark the conference's tenth year of providing over $11,000 yearly in educational scholarships and programs offering encouragement and mentoring. Kathy also serves as administrative executive director of Internal Hope Fellowship located in Friendswood, TX.

In 2009, Kathy was honored with the Cheryl Crummie *Esther Award* for excellence and distinction in ministry presented by Dr. Lois Evans, host and founder of *the First Lady Conference (The Urban Alternative)* and in 2006 was recipient of the Gloria Peterson Scholarship award.

Kathy attended North Texas State University (now University of North Texas) and San Jacinto College. A classical pianist, she is also an alumnus of the Billy Graham School of Evangelism, and certified teacher through Child Evangelism Fellowship.

Kathy and her husband/favorite pastor George Sr. have three adult sons, two daughters-in-love, and six beautiful grandchildren.

Clayton Catchings

Founder & Chairman
National Afro-American
Corvette Club

Clayton Catchings is founder and chairman of the National Afro-American Corvette Club (NAACC). The NAACC is the first nationwide club bringing African Americans together to enjoy the hobby and is a social club with chapters in Houston, Philadelphia and New York/New Jersey. Activities in the nonprofit organization include cruises, car shows, picnics, parades, parties and charitable giving. A shelter for children of incarcerated parents and local community centers are the primary recipients of charitable support.

Clayton is also chairman of the Corvette Clubs of Greater Houston, a committee of representatives from the major Corvette Clubs in the Houston Metropolis.

He attended school in Houston and joined the U.S. Army in 1969. After nine years in the military and a tour in southeast Asia, Clayton returned to Houston, enrolled in Texas Southern University graduating, with honors, in 1982, and subsequently accepting a position with ExxonMobil.

Clayton retired from ExxonMobil as a credit manager in 2003. A member of Wheeler Avenue Baptist Church, Clayton serves as staff photographer. He and his wife, Victoria, have three children and five grandchildren.

For nearly two decades, Paul D. Charles has led Neighborhood Recovery Community Development Corporation in the development and redevelopment of commercial real estate and affordable housing projects.

Paul holds a Bachelor of Science degree in civil engineering from Northwestern University and a Master of Business Administration degree from the Tuck School at Dartmouth College. He completed executive education at the Harvard Kennedy School, and is a registered professional engineer in California.

He is a member of Wheeler Avenue Baptist Church, past president of the Houston Chapter of the National Black MBA Association and a member of Leadership Houston Class XVIII. He is on the executive committee of Scenic Houston, and a board member of Urban Harvest Inc. and the Tuck Alumni Advisory Program. He is also a member of community advisory board of Comerica Bank and chairman of the Third Ward Redevelopment Council.

Paul has received numerous awards including the Outstanding Young Men of America and the Leadership Award from the American Legion.

He enjoys spending time with family and friends, eating good food and has photographed his way across all seven continents.

Paul D. Charles

Executive Director
Neighborhood Recovery
Community Development Corporation

Elmer Donalson-Rogers is director of fund development for the Houston Area Urban League. She is responsible for managing general and operational development needs for the organization. Since 1999 she has been responsible for implementing annual funding initiatives, which include major gift solicitation, event coordination and capital campaign fund raising.

Elmer is very active in the Greater Houston community, as well as her church and has traveled to Haiti on several mission trips. She was the winner of the Ethnographic Research and Writing Award from the Texas Southern University Department of Communications and served as delegate to the state department sponsored round table at the Air Force Academy "World Affairs – Asia and Japan." She currently sits on the boards of Grant Writers Network of Greater Houston and Houston Museum of African American Culture.

Donaldson-Rogers received a bachelor's degree in public affairs with a minor in political science and core in international relations from Texas Southern University.

A native of Dallas, Texas, Donaldon-Rogers is the mother of one son, Rev. Kevin E. Donalson Sr.

Elmer Donalson-Rogers

Director of Fund Development
Houston Area Urban League

Cheryl Lacey Donovan

Founder & Chief Visionary Officer
Worth More than Rubies Ministries

As an award-winning author, Bible teacher, ordained minister and evangelist, Cheryl Donovan's message is not only meant to entertain, but to minister to and encourage others.

As founder and president of Worth More Than Rubies Ministries in Houston, Texas, Cheryl teaches on hundreds of subjects, has authored several books and conducts conferences throughout the year. She also has a radio program, *Titus 2 Tuesdays*, which is broadcast worldwide via the internet each week. In 2010 Cheryl's ministry became overseer of four churches organized in Kenya.

Cheryl is a recipient of a 2009 African American Literary Award and columnist for *Gospel Truth Magazine*. She has spoken to thousands of people in major cities nationwide, is a 17 year teaching veteran and has presented for and or been profiled by such organizations as Prairie View A&M University School of Nursing, The National Black Book Festival, *The North Dallas Gazette*, *Great Day Houston*, Heaven 1580 and *The Reading Circle with Marc Medley* on WP88.7 FM.

Donovan lives in Houston with her husband Keith. They are the proud parents of three adult children and grandparents to two grandsons.

Tiffany Dorsey

Individual Development Director
Big Brothers Big Sisters
of Greater Houston

Tiffany Dorsey is individual development director for Big Brothers Big Sisters of Greater Houston, a donor-funded volunteer organization that enhances the lives of children through one-to-one mentoring relationships. In this position, Dorsey manages a comprehensive, annual giving program centered on contributions from individual donors. She has been responsible for implementing the annual funding initiative since 2008 and focuses on major gift solicitations.

Dorsey received a bachelor's degree from Lamar University in Beaumont, where she served as secretary for the regional chapter of the National Society of Black Engineers. A member of the Association of Fundraising Professionals and the Houston Black Professionals, she is an advisor to the Big Brothers Big Sisters of Greater Houston Black Professionals Mentoring Group. In addition, Dorsey is an active member of New Light Christian Center Church, where she serves as a greeter, spiritual motivator and teen ministry volunteer.

A native of Port Arthur, Texas, she is the wife of Dorie Dorsey and a proud mother of two daughters, Ashley and Lyric.

Anthony Freddie is management analyst for Houston Police Department, Neighborhood Protection Division. In this role, he manages constituent issues and resource resolution for elective officials, community leaders and other city department(s). Anthony has created and managed community based projects, the City Council Cleanup (C3 Program), a program developed to stabilize target stressed communities plagued with blight, and other unwanted eyesores, reducing negative elements, received the Mayor's Prod Partner Award.

Anthony currently serves as first vice president-Houston Chapter, National Forum for Black Public Administrators, Director of the World Youth Foundation, Empowering Youth Initiative, A CHILD'S WALK Program, and chair of Rebuild together Houston Senior Home Repair Program, received 2006 Golden Hammer Award.

A native of Houston, Texas, Anthony is single and a proud father.

Anthony Freddie

Management Analyst
Houston Police Department

Jean Gabriel is founder and chief executive officer of P.U.S.H. TO W.I.N. (Pray Until Something Happens to Walk in Newness) OUTREACH, INC. P.U.S.H. targets the Sunnyside area because of the effect that poverty and disease have had on youth in the area.

P.U.S.H. has partnered with schools and apartment complexes to provide youth and families educational, motivational, emotional and social support programs. The goal is to help the Sunnyside community overcome the difficulties associated with poverty and disease by showing and teaching Christian-based love.

Jean was employed at KETH-TV 14, an affiliate of TBN, where she was the coordinator of *Praise the Lord* and the producer of *Joy In Our Town*. She is now in ministry full time.

Jean has received recognition from community leaders for her service and devotion to the community including a congressional letter of support from Congressman Al Green and the recipient of the Susan Taylor's Mentoring Award.

A native of Indianapolis, Indiana, Jean is the wife of Amos Gabriel. She has four daughters, Amonee', Goldie, Angela and Lillian. and three granddaughters.

Jean Gabriel

Founder & CEO
P.U.S.H. TO WIN OUTREACH, INC.

Katrina R. Johnson

Chief Executive Officer & Founder
Horizon Outreach

Katrina Johnson is the chief executive officer and founder of Horizon Outreach, a non-profit 501 (c) 3 organization whose mission is *to give the homeless a new start*. The mission is accomplished through several programs that increase self-sufficiency and self-esteem. The FAITH program (Families Achieving Independence Through Help) connects clients to life skills training, career counseling, food/clothing, housing and other resources. The primary focus group is military veterans and their families. In less than one year the organization has connected over 700 clients to resources within the community.

Johnson is also the Broker/Owner of K. Johnson Realty, a premiere real estate firm that assists clients in buying, leasing and selling their homes in Houston and surrounding areas. She is a HUD approved broker experienced in pre-foreclosure sales. In addition, she serves on the Houston Homeless Coalition's Leadership Council and as the Council Secretary for the Harris County Hospital District's Health Care for the Homeless Council.

Johnson is a 2009 graduate of Auburn University's Executive MBA Program.

Paul J. Matthews

Founder & Executive Director
Buffalo Soldiers National Museum

Paul J. Matthews is founder and executive director of the Buffalo Soldiers National Museum, the only museum in the United States that chronicles the entire African-American military experience from the Revolutionary War to the Persian Gulf War. He has been researching military history, and collecting military artifacts and memorabilia for more than 33 years.

Currently, more than 60 percent of the museum's collection has been donated from Matthews' private collection. A former captain in the U.S. Army, he received a Bronze Star Medal and Combat Medical Badge in the Republic of Vietnam in 1969. He went on to become executive business manager and director of military affairs for Merck & Co., Inc.

Matthews is a recipient of the Congressional Black Caucus' Veterans' Braintrust Award, the National Education Association's Carter G. Woodson Award and an NAACP Community Service Award.

A graduate of Prairie View A&M University, Matthews is a life member of Kappa Alpha Psi Fraternity, Inc. and a member of Fort Bend Church. He and his wife, Barbara, have one son and two grandsons.

Rev. Byron C. Stevenson is the pastor and founder of The Fort Bend Church. The church was founded on August 1, 2004 at Sugar Land Middle School in Sugar Land, Texas. Over 600 individuals attended and joined. Since that time the church has grown to over 3,000 members.

Stevenson is a member of Alpha Phi Alpha Fraternity, Inc. He is also a life member of the Southern University Alumni Association. Stevenson is a member of the executive board of the Baptist General Convention of Texas. He has also served as secretary for the African American Pastor's Fellowship of Texas.

Pastor Stevenson graduated from Southern University in 1990 with a Bachelor of Science degree in accounting. He received a Masters of Arts degree in theological studies from Houston Baptist University in 2006.

A native of Baton Rouge, Louisiana, Stevenson is the husband of Sonya Taylor Stevenson and the proud father of two daughters, Claire Alexandra and Cydney Victoria.

Rev. Byron C. Stevenson

Senior Pastor
The Fort Bend Church

Dr. Vernus C. Swisher is chief executive officer of Career and Recovery Resources, Inc., a nonprofit United Way agency established in 1945 that helps people identify and overcome barriers to employment.

Vern retired from the retail industry with more than 25 years experience in merchandising as a Foley's (now Macy's) store manager. His public sector experience includes more than 25 years as a United Way volunteer. His nonprofit leadership includes serving as executive director of Julia C. Hester House. He is an ordained minister and pastor of Galilee Community Baptist Church in Houston.

A native Texan who is committed to the Houston community, he serves on the boards of the College of Biblical Studies, the Houston Graduate School of Theology, the PrimeWay Federal Credit Union and the Mid-Town Management District. Vern is past president of the Rotary Club of Houston and the assistant governor in District 5890. He is one of the founders of Leadership Houston, Project Blueprint, and a senior fellow with the American Leadership Forum.

Vern and his wife, Alma, are blessed with three adult children and one grandson.

Dr. Vernus C. Swisher

Chief Executive Officer
Career and Recovery Resources, Inc.

Jackie C. Thomas Jr.

Chief Executive Officer & Founder
The Foundation for Student
Leadership and Success

As the Chief Executive Officer and founder of the Foundation for Student Leadership and Success (FSLS), Jackie C. Thomas Jr. is committed to developing mature, college-ready student leaders that will make a positive impact in their respective communities. The FSLS provides programming that exposes underserved high school students to the concepts of servant leadership, individual responsibility, and college preparedness. In 2010, the Foundation for Student Leadership and Success was recognized as one of the Houston Independent School District's Community Partners of the Year.

In addition to providing leadership for the FSLS, Jackie is currently pursuing a Doctor of Philosophy degree in educational psychology and individual differences. His areas of research include academic motivation, persistence, and retention among minority college students.

Jackie serves on the board of directors for the University of Houston Black Alumni Association, The B-Side, and is involved with Big Brothers Big Sisters, the Houston Real Men Read Program, and the LeaderShape Institute.

He received a Bachelor of Science degree in consumer science and Merchandising from the University of Houston in 2004 and a Master of Science degree in higher education from Florida State University in 2006.

Sherrie Zeno

Business Development Manager
Women's Business Enterprise Alliance

Sherrie Zeno is business development manager for the Women's Business Enterprise Alliance (WBEA), where she manages aspects of the nonprofit's public relations, marketing and business development efforts. During her tenure with WBEA, Sherrie was recognized by the president of the board of directors for her outstanding public speaking abilities.

Prior to joining WBEA, Sherrie worked as a corporate training human resource manager for ExpressJet Airlines, Inc., and held the position of senior diversity analyst at Continental Airlines, Inc., for more than 13 years. Sherrie's strengths and passion is in helping business professionals and entrepreneurs to succeed by delivering innovative trainings programs, powerful business development influences and structured marketing strategies.

Sherrie has studied at the Rice University Susan M. Glasscock School and Houston Community College. She has an associate degree in business management and a human resources certification. She is a current member of the Society for Human Resource Management, HR Houston and the Greater Houston Partnership. She is a member of the 2011 NCAA Final Four Houston Local Organizing Committee and also an avid supporter of Avondale House.

Houston's PROFESSIONALS

KNOWLEDGEABLE

QUALIFIED

SPECIALIST

PROFICIENT

GURU

DILIGENT

SKILLFUL

COMPETENT

PRECISE

Tinya Taylor Bassett

Realtor
Realty Associates

Tinya Taylor Bassett first pursued a career as a program director for disabled adults. With a master's degree in sociology, this was a perfect match. After several years working with disabled adults, she opted for a new challenge. Tinya became a licensed real estate agent.

Tinya is committed to offering her clients the highest quality representation and professionalism, as well as complete confidentiality, patience and diligence. She remains committed to personal and professional growth, while enhancing the real estate experience for her clients.

Tinya is also an instructor at Lonestar College, where she teaches sociology.

Tinya has an undergraduate degree in criminal justice from the University of Houston, where she also received her master's degree. Her professional memberships include membership and past co-chair of Alpha Kappa Delta Sorority, Inc., the Sociology Honor Society, the Houston Association of Realtors, the Texas Association of Realtors and the National Association of Realtors. She is the wife of Anthony Bassett.

Thomasina Burns

Regional Manager
Community Health Charities Texas

Thomasina Burns is the regional manager for Community Health Charities Texas. In this position, she is responsible for cultivating relationships with corporate partners and facilitating charitable contributions in the workplace. She also consults with companies on how to improve employee engagement and promote workplace access to the services of the health charities she represents.

Thomasina was a 2010 participant of the American Express Non-Profit Leadership Academy. She also serves on the board of directors of Expressions Productions Dance Company, which is dedicated to furthering the choreographic skills of its young dancers and offer regularly programs for youth, workshops and competitions.

Thomasina received a Bachelor of Science degree from Lamar University and currently seeking a Master in Business Administration degree from Columbia Southern University.

A native Houstonian, Thomasina is the wife of Kendal Burns and the proud mother of Kendal Burns Jr. She enjoys actively participating in various ministries in her church and volunteering in the community in which she lives.

Graduating from Booker T. Washington High School in 1948, Lorenza Butler entered Texas College in Tyler on a football scholarship. In 1950 he transferred to Texas Southern University. After receiving a bachelor's degree, he was drafted into the U.S. Army.

Butler began coaching in Dickinson, Texas, at Paul Laurence Dunbar High School in 1956. He received a master's degree from TSU in 1961. When completely integrated, he was an assistant football coach at Dickinson High School and basketball. In 1970 he came to Lamar Fleming Junior High School.

Butler became a Harris County constable at Precinct 6 in the 1970s. He later became a coach for the Houston Police Department as special teams coach for the Houston Gunners and he still coaches for them.

A member of Metropolitan CME Church, Butler is former chairman of Eastex Wholesale Beer, Inc., president emeritus of the Informer and the Texas Freeman newspapers and radio stations. He is a 1949 Gamma Alpha initiate of Alpha Phi Alpha Fraternity, Inc. Butler is married to Hilda Butler, and they have eight children, eight grandchildren and five great-grandchildren.

Lorenza Phillips Butler Jr.

Chairman & Chief Executive Officer
Freedmen's Publishing Company

Byron Cherry is an attorney in the Energy Transactions/Projects practice group of Vinson & Elkins, focusing on domestic and international energy-related business transactions and project development. He has represented clients and has experience in various industries, including energy, financial services and consumer products, working on matters in the U.S., Europe, Asia and Australia. In 2008 he was selected for *Texas Monthly* magazine's Super Lawyers–Rising Stars Edition, and in 2009 he was named a Professional on the Fast Track in *H Texas Magazine*.

A graduate of St. John's School, Byron earned a Bachelor of Science degree in economics from the Wharton School of the University of Pennsylvania and a juris doctorate degree, cum laude, from the University of Florida College of Law.

Before law school, Byron served for four years as an officer in the United States Marine Corps, achieving the rank of captain.

A native Houstonian, Byron is married to Reena W. Cherry and they have one daughter, Ava. He is a member of the board of trustees of St. John's School and Omega Psi Phi Fraternity, Inc.

Byron C. Cherry

Associate, Attorney at Law
Vinson & Elkins LLP

Joel Clary

General Sales Manager
Radio One Houston

Joel Clary is the general sales manager of the two powerhouse radio stations serving the African American community in the Houston/Galveston area, Majic 102.1 and Praise 92.1. He manages the day to day operations of the sales and marketing efforts of advertising. Joel's responsibilities consist of keeping the advertising community informed of the necessity of reaching the African American consumer when placing media and to insure that the audience is being represented in a positive light with discretionary spending power.

Joel is a member of the Omega Psi Phi Fraternity, Inc., a member of 100 Black Men of Houston and sits on the board for the Texas Black Expo.

He attended the University of Missouri concentrating his studies on broadcast journalism.

Joel is married to his beautiful wife Tonya with three wonderful children, daughter Chloe, stepdaughter Tia and stepson Kian.

Keith J. Davis Sr.

Owner & Chief Executive Officer
d-mars.com

Keith J. Davis Sr., also known as "Mr. D-Mars," is owner and chief executive officer of d-mars.com. He has been in the marketing and communications industry for many years, starting out as a marketing consultant and evolving into a marketing guru. In 2010 d-mars.com celebrated its 11-year anniversary as the premier African-American marketing and communications firm in the Houston area.

The website specializes in image marketing, business consulting, franchising/business opportunities, supplier diversity support, the Discount Partner Program, graphic design, website design and full-color printing. In addition, it offers advertising with the monthly *d-mars.com Business Journal*, the *Black Pages* business directory, business connections and promotional items.

D-mars.com knows technology is changing and the world wide web is where it is at.

R od Evans is a freelance journalist and the editor in chief of Houston-based *Health & Fitness Sports Magazine*, a 26-year-old, monthly, 50,000-circulation publication.

During his tenure as editor, the publication has earned a reputation as one of Houston's leading sources for consumer news and information on health, wellness, fitness and recreational sports. The publication has garnered numerous national, regional and local awards, including from the Texas Medical Association and the National Health Information Resource Center.

Prior to joining the staff of *Health & Fitness Sports Magazine*, Evans worked in the radio industry for 15 years as a news/sports reporter, anchor and talk show host. Evans' freelance articles have appeared in *Autoweek*, *Oxygen* and TheSportingnews.com. He is also an active web content writer.

Rod earned a Bachelor of Arts degree from the University of North Texas. He is a member of the Houston Association of Black Journalists and the Society for Professional Journalists.

A native of Houston, Rod is married to Wendy and is a stepfather to three children, ages 14, 17 and 28.

Rod Evans

Editor In Chief
Health & Fitness Sports Magazine

S helia Fleming is the Sweetwater Division package division manager at UPS Inc. Her team manages more than 600 hourly employees and an average daily volume of approximately 87,000 packages.

She started her career as an administrative assistant in the finance and accounting department in Jackson, Mississippi. She was promoted to a service provider where she remained until 2004. Shelia received a promotion to an on-car supervisor in Jackson Metro center. In 2007, Shelia relocated to Gray, Louisiana where she was promoted as a business manager in the Houma Center. Shelia accepted a special assignment in 2010 to the Stafford facility as the business manager in the Lakeside center. In January 2011, Shelia and her family relocated to Houston, Texas.

Shelia holds a bachelor's degree in social science education and a master's degree in adult education and training.

Shelia, and her husband Theo, have four children, Zac, Denzel, Tia and Tamera.

Shelia Fleming

Sweetwater Package Division Manager
UPS

Kimberly Floyd

Regional Manager
rolling out

Kimberly Floyd is a regional manager for *rolling out*, the largest chain of black weekly newspapers in the country. In this position, she manages advertising, event promotions and marketing campaigns for the newspaper in Dallas, Houston and New Orleans. Kim is the producer of the Top 25 Women of Houston, an annual event that honors top executives, entrepreneurs and nonprofit and civic leaders in Houston. She also produces Seeding Minds, a children's literacy event aimed at empowering today's youth.

Kim has received numerous awards for her service, including a Special Recognition award from the mayor of Dallas in 2007. She is currently a member of the Houston Chapter of the National Black MBA Association and the Houston Area Urban League.

Kim received a Bachelor of Science degree in economics from Texas Woman's University and Master of Business Administration degree from the University of Dallas.

Courteney Harris

Attorney at Law
Aldine Independent School District

Courteney Harris is an attorney for Aldine Independent School District. Her primary duty entails litigation of tax matters. She has also participated in hearings before the Texas Education Agency. Harris has been an adjunct professor at The University of Phoenix for eight years. She was named Faculty of the Year by The University of Phoenix's Graduate and Business Management Department. The award is based on student feedback and assessments by the administrative staff.

Harris received a Bachelor of Arts degree from Xavier University in New Orleans. She received a master's degree in public administration with a specialization in human resources and juris doctorate degree from Texas Southern University. She is a member of Delta Sigma Theta, Inc.

Debra Gatison Hatter is a partner in the corporate practice group. Her practice focuses on mergers and acquisitions, corporate securities, joint ventures and strategic partnerships including, HSR compliance, investment funds, corporate governance and general business matters in a range of industries. Companies in the Fortune 500 as well as startups are included among Debra's clients.

Debra is an advisory board member of Youth About Business, former board member of the Houston Area Urban League and a founder and past chair of the Houston Bar Association's Mergers and Acquisitions Section.

Debra has been voted a SuperLawyer by *Texas Monthly* magazine and executive volunteer of the year by Youth About Business.

A native of Connecticut, Debra received her law degree from the University of Pennsylvania Law School and her undergraduate degree in mechanical engineering from the University of Pennsylvania School of Engineering and Applied Science.

Debra G. Hatter

Partner, Attorney at Law
Haynes and Boone, LLP

Constance Y. Jones is director of membership services for the Houston Minority Business Council, serving as the liaison between the council and minority business owners. She is responsible for the recruitment, retention, certification and orientation of all minority business enterprises. She ensures these owners are informed regarding various programs, services and technical support opportunities.

Constance has received several awards and acknowledgments for her dedication and support to minority business development. She has appeared in several media outlets discussing issues facing minority entrepreneurship. She was also named the General Services Administration Small Business Advocate of the Year and the U.S. Small Business Advocate of the Year.

Constance earned a bachelor's degree in business administration and in political science from the University of Southern California. She is a member of several community and civic organizations, including Alpha Kappa Alpha Sorority, Inc. and the YMCA Young Entrepreneurial Program. Prior to joining the council's staff, Constance worked as a management consultant in the private sector conducting and maintaining research on specific strategic alliances, as well as exploring cultural change philosophy.

Constance Y. Jones

Director of Membership Services
Houston Minority Business Council

Devika Kornbacher

Attorney at Law
Vinson & Elkins LLP

D evika Kornbacher is an associate in the Intellectual Property Practice Group at Vinson & Elkins where she practices intellectual property law in the context of business transactions. She has co-authored a paper entitled "Privilege and the Scope of Waiver Regarding Opinions of Counsel after EchoStar," which was published by the University of Texas School of Law Advanced Patent Law Institute.

Before practicing law, Devika designed offshore oil and gas platforms located in the Gulf of Mexico and off the coast of Nigeria. Today, Devika enjoys bringing her previous experience to the forefront by counseling clients in the sale, acquisition and marketing of energy-related technologies.

Devika received a Bachelor of Science degree in civil engineering, with honors, from the University of Houston and a juris doctorate degree from Harvard Law School, where she served as the technology director for the student-run Harvard Legal Aid Bureau. In 2005, Ford Motor Company awarded Devika a scholarship for her leadership in her law school and the community.

James E. Phillips

Attorney at Law
Baker Hostetler LLP

J ames Phillips is a trial lawyer who focuses his practice in the areas of complex commercial litigation, products liability, consumer issues, collection matters, premises liability, construction litigation and oil and gas litigation.

Phillips represented a number of automobile manufacturers that are subject to state and federal warranty laws and consumer protection statutes. He has taken over 300 of these cases to resolution and successfully defended one such case before the State Office of Administrative Hearings. Additionally, Phillips has obtained summary judgment on a number of these cases by successfully challenging the plaintiff's status as a consumer under the Moss Magnuson Act and Texas Deceptive Trade Practices Act.

Phillips was a member of the University of Texas Moot Court Team. He participated in the annual moot court competitions hosted by the American Bar Association and Texas Young Lawyers' Association and earned several speaking and team awards.

Phillips is a member of the Texas and Houston Bar Associations and the Texas and Houston Young Lawyers' Associations.

J Goodwille Pierre is the manager of the Small Business Development and Contract Compliance Division of the Houston Airport System and an adjunct patent law professor at the Thurgood Marshall School of Law. He previously served as district director for Congresswoman Sheila Jackson Lee.

A national board member at large for the National Bar Association, Pierre is also a member of 100 Black Men of Metro Houston. Additionally, he is a member of Omega Psi Phi Fraternity, Inc. and the NAACP.

Pierre attended Morehouse College and Georgia State University, earning a bachelor's degree in chemistry, with a minor in physics. He earned a master's degree from the University of Central Florida and a juris doctorate degree from South Texas College of Law. Pierre is licensed with the Supreme Court of Texas, The Federal Southern District of Texas and the United States Patent and Trademark Office.

He is married to his wonderful wife of 16 years, Jacquelyn Tinsley, a native of Houston, and has two beautiful daughters, Joi Candace and Jada Elaine.

J. Goodwille Pierre

Manager
Small Business Development
& Contract Compliance Division

D avid Rainey has been in the Alley Theatre Resident Company since 2000. Regionally he has performed for the Guthrie Theatre, Joseph Papp Public Theatre, Steppenwolf Theatre Company, the National Actors Theatre, Crossroads Theatre Company, New York Shakespeare Festival, Hartford Stage, Berkeley Rep, Repertory Theatre of St. Louis, Ford's Theatre, Asolo Theatre, Manhattan Theatre Club, and Houston Grand Opera, among others. Some film and television credits include *Law & Order*, *Cosby*, *Vengeance Unlimited*, *Lowball*, *Star Force*, *As the World Turns*, and *One Life to Live*.

David is also artist director of The Landing Theatre Company, and has been an adjunct professor at University of Houston-Downtown since 2005, where he was its first resident artist in drama. He is a graduate of ENMU and The Juilliard School, where he received the Drama Division's highest honor, the Michel and Suria Saint-Denis prize.

David Rainey

Resident Artist
Alley Theatre

Tiko Reynolds-Hausman

Compliance and Program Advisor Manager
Office of Small Business
Metropolitan Transit Authority

Tiko Reynolds-Hausman is the compliance and program advisor manager for METRO. In this position, she determines needs and develops technical assistance planning for METRO's Small and Disadvantaged Business Enterprise Program. Tiko serves as liaison between METRO Procurement and Office of Small Business to identify small businesses and generate small business participation in METRO procurements.

Tiko has been nominated for advocate of the year twice by the Women's Business Enterprise Alliance. Tiko was the first founding member of the Texas Business Enterprise Alliance and is an active committee member of the annual Government Procurement Connections (GPC) Conference and Conference of Minority Transportation Officials (COMTO).

Tiko holds a Bachelor of Arts degree in English from the University of Houston-Downtown.

A native of Dallas, Tiko is the wife of Ray Hausman and proud mother of Zoey Love and Wynton Xavier. Tiko is an advent foodie who enjoys reading and traveling with her family.

Brendetta Anthony Scott

Attorney at Law
Hughes, Watters & Askanase, LLP

Brendetta Anthony Scott is counsel for Hughes, Watters & Askanase, LLP. She focuses her practice on creditors' rights, bankruptcy, eviction and foreclosure litigation, representing various mortgage companies and credit unions.

Brendetta, a certified mediator, was a federal bankruptcy judge's invitee to the 63rd Judicial Conference of the Fifth Circuit Judges in May 2009. She was voted as a Rising Star in the area of bankruptcy law in 2007, 2008 and 2010 by her colleagues. Also, she is a frequent speaker for attorney CLE activities, including speaking at the State Bar's Advanced Consumer Bankruptcy Seminar (2010), University of Texas' Consumer Bankruptcy Practice Seminar (2008-2010), University of Houston School of Law's Collecting Debts & Judgments Seminar (2007-2008) and the Southern District of Texas' Bench Bar Conference (2008). Brendetta has also served as a member of the Law Week Committee (2006-2007 co-chair) and the Professionalism Committee of the Houston Bar Association, where she served as co-chair (2008-2009).

Brendetta received a juris doctorate degree from Texas Southern University, Thurgood Marshall School of Law, with honors, and a bachelor's degree from Jackson State University, where she graduated, magna cum laude.

Renita L. Scroggins is a full-time licensed realtor with RE/MAX Top Realty. Her goal is to help her clients gain wealth through the sale and acquisition of real estate property. Her areas of specialization include first-time homebuyers, move-up buyers, distressed property sellers and property management.

Named a 2011 Five Star Real Estate Agent based on client satisfaction featured in *Texas Monthly* magazine, Renita also serves as a Pearland Chamber of Commerce director, PTA executive board member, a member of the Houston Citizens Chamber of Commerce and is a lifetime member of the National Black MBA Association– Houston Chapter, where she has served as scholarship banquet co-chair and secretary.

Renita received a Bachelor of Science degree in environmental engineering from Northwestern University in Evanston, Illinois, and was awarded a Master of Business Administration from the University of St. Thomas in Houston. She holds accredited buyers representative, certified residential Specialist and certified distressed property expert designations.

A native of Shreveport, Louisiana, Renita is the wife of Warren Scroggins and the proud mother of two beautiful daughters, Kaitlyn and Kamryn.

Renita L. Scroggins

Real Estate Specialist
RE/MAX Top Realty

Kimberly Shoaf is the regional human resources manager for ARAMARK. Kimberly has more than 15 years of experience in human resources, energy, transportation, beverage and document management industries. Her responsibilities include the Western Region, which consists of 11 states. She oversees strategic planning, organizational effectiveness initiatives and intellectual capital.

Kimberly is currently a member of HR Houston and the Society for Human Resource Management. Additionally, she is one of the founding members of the National Association of African Americans in Human Resources. She is a member of Delta Sigma Theta Sorority, Inc. and sits on the executive board of the Texas Democratic Women of Harris County Metro Area. Kimberly served on the board of the National Black MBA Association, Brentwood Community Foundation Scholarship Committee advisory board, National Coalition of 100 Black Women, AIDS Foundation Houston, Career Recovery Resources Advisory Council and the United Negro College Fund.

Kimberly is a certified human resources professional. She holds a Bachelor of Science degree from Texas State University in San Marcos and a Master of Science degree from the University of Houston.

Kimberly Shoaf

Regional Human Resources Manager
ARAMARK

Rachel Smith

Attorney at Law
Baker Hostetler LLP

Rachel Smith is an attorney representing management in a number of industries on employment matters in state and federal court and before administrative agencies, including the Equal Employment Opportunity Commission, Department of Labor and Texas Workforce Commission. Rachel regularly drafts employment agreements and policies, counsels and trains on best practices involving the employer-employee relationship. Rachel speaks and writes on employment law, including managing workplace technology, international workforces, avoiding claims, and ending hostile work environments.

Rachel was named a Texas Rising Star by *Texas Monthly and Law and Politics* in 2010 and 2011.

Rachel received a Bachelor of Arts degree from Baylor University and a law degree from the University of Texas School of Law. During law school, she was a member of the Texas Journal of Business Law and a regional champion in the National Black Law Student Association's Thurgood Marshall Mock Trial Competition. She served as an attorney ad litem in the Children's Rights Clinic. She is a member of the Federal, Texas and Houston Bar associations.

She and her husband Michael, are proud parents of a daughter, Olivia.

Gregory C. Ulmer

Attorney at Law
Baker Hostetler LLP

Gregory C. Ulmer is a trial lawyer who represents clients in wrongful death, general tort litigation, premises liability, and product liability matters. Ulmer has extensive experience litigating in federal and state courts, as well as before arbitration panels.

In addition to his substantial litigation experience, Ulmer also has primary responsibility for managing mass tort litigation. He currently serves as chair of Baker Hostetler's Product Liability/Toxic Tort Practice Group.

Ulmer has been consistently recognized as a "Super Lawyer Rising Star" by *Texas Monthly* magazine. He is very active in local and state bar activities. He currently serves on the Houston Bar Foundation Board of Directors. In addition, he served as a board member on the Houston Bar Association's Board of Directors for eight years. During that time, he chaired numerous committees and task forces, including serving as president of the Houston Lawyers Referral Service, Inc.

Texas Governor Rick Perry recently reappointed Ulmer to the Texas Board of Professional Geoscientists. He previously served as chair of the Houston Police Officers Civil Service Commission.

Pamela Ulmer is an industrial relations advisor for Aramco Services Company (ASC). ASC is the U.S.-based subsidiary of the world's largest oil producing and exporting company, Saudi Aramco. ASC provides a wide range of support to Saudi Aramco, including career development programs and training opportunities for Saudi Aramco sponsored students. Pamela is responsible for the placement of more than 200 sponsored students every year to universities throughout North America.

Pamela currently serves on the board for the Houston Area Urban League. In the Houston community she serves as co-chair for Act One, the ensemble theatre's professional group and on the advisory committee for the Houston Grand Opera's Opening Nights (HGO). Pamela is an active member of Brookhollow Baptist Church and Alpha Kappa Alpha Sorority Inc.

In 2009 Pamela was awarded HGO's Ovation Award, which recognizes professionals in the realm of philanthropic, charitable and civic endeavors.

A native of Erie, Pennsylvania, Pamela attended Penn State University earning a bachelor's degree in psychology and a Master of Education degree in counseling education.

Pamela A. Ulmer

Industrial Relations Advisor
Aramco Services Company

Lavon Washington is a senior associate in the Houston office of Mercer Inc. He is responsible for client satisfaction with all services provided by Mercer. As a Mercer consultant, Washington helps clients design and manage health, retirement and other benefits and optimize human capital. The firm also provides customized administration, technology and total benefit outsourcing solutions.

Washington volunteers in his community and has served on the executive board of the National Black MBA Association Houston Chapter. He is currently a mentor for the organization's high school mentoring program, Leaders of Tomorrow (LOT) and coached the winning LOT National Case Competition team in 2005.

Washington received a Bachelor of Science degree in computer information systems from the University of Nebraska-Kearney in 2001, and a Master of Business Administration degree from Rice University in 2006. He also founded the first black business student organization at his alma mater, Rice University.

A native of Shreveport, Louisiana, and raised in Houston, Texas, Washington enjoys traveling, reading and working out. He is the son of Cheryl Washington and has two younger brothers, Lavelle and Aaron.

Lavon Washington

Senior Associate
Mercer Inc.

Michael A. Williams

Manager
Wortham Theater Center

Michael A. Williams is the manager of Houston's most noted premier performing arts facility and architectural landmark, the Wortham Theater Center. He is responsible for the daily operations and administration of the venue. He and his team create a theater experience second to none.

Michael is the president of the Alpha Eta Lambda Chapter of Alpha Phi Alpha Fraternity, Inc. Leading the third largest chapter in the fraternity, the chapter was named the 2010 International Outstanding Alumni Chapter of the Year. He also serves on the Time and Place Committee at the district and regional levels.

Michael is a member of the International Association of Assembly Managers, the International Facilities Management Association, the 100 Black Men of Metropolitan Houston, and the National Black MBA Association.

Michael received his Bachelor of Business Administration degree from the University of North Texas and earned a Master of Business Administration degree from Prairie View A&M University. A member of the Lilly Grove Baptist Church, he's committed to providing scholarship opportunities to deserving students.

Houston's YOUTH ACHIEVERS

PROFICIENT

EXCEL

OUTSHINE

SURPASS

TRANSCEND

ENHANCE

SURMOUNT

MASTER

TRIUMPH

Allahjah Johne Brown

Sophomore
Michael E. DeBakey High School
for Health Professions

Allahjah Johne Brown is a sophomore who attends Michael E. DeBakey High School for Health Professions. She maintains a 3.75 GPA and is an honor roll student. She looks forward to attending Harvard University and/or Baylor College of Medicine after graduation for her pre-medicine studies and medical school.

Allahjah has aspired to find a cure for cancer since she was in elementary school and plans to have a medical career as an Oncologist.

In addition to being a second year member of Leaders of Tomorrow, she is a member of the Christian Student Union, Desi Cultural Club, Vietnamese International Student Association, Organization of Latin America, and yearbook staff at DeBakey HSHP. She has completed 100 volunteer hours at the nearby YMCA after school program working with children from her former elementary school.

Because it is important to her to be a well-rounded individual, she has participated in, and been rewarded in, dance and spirit team since middle school. She attends Windsor Village United Methodist Church with her family. Allahjah's proud parents are Kristina Tyler and Royalton Brown.

Farrah Robyn Fisher

Senior
Stephen F. Austin High School

Farrah Robyn Fisher is a senior at Stephen F. Austin High School in Fort Bend County. She is a writer for her school's yearbook staff, *The Onyx*, and plays on the Lady Bulldog Varsity Basketball Team.

Farrah's most recent accomplishments include placing first with her team in the NBMBAA Leaders of Tomorrow Local Case Competition and being featured in the 2011 *Who's Who Magazine*.

She has two sisters and lives with her parents, Robert and Brenda Fisher, in Sugar Land, Texas. In the fall of 2011, Farrah plans to major in business marketing/advertising at either Texas State University or the University of North Texas. Farrah is a member of Windsor Village United Methodist Church and some of her hobbies include traveling, playing sports, dancing and spending time with family and friends.

D errick Kent II is a sophomore at Mirabeau B. Lamar High School. He is active in the Leaders of Tomorrow (LOT) high school mentoring program, and plays on a local basketball team. Derrick has also served as captain of the Lamar Junior Varsity Basketball Team.

Derrick aspires to become a lawyer or fighter pilot in the U.S. Air Force. His college preferences are the USC, Air Force Academy in Colorado Springs, Florida A&M University, or the University of Missouri. Derrick attends St. Johns Baptist church, and is the son of Mandisa Gibson and Derrick Kent.

Derrick Kent II

Sophomore
Mirabeau B. Lamar High School

J eremy D. Simmons is a senior at Lamar Consolidated High School. He is a member of the National Honor Society and Distributive Education Clubs of America (DECA).

Jeremy was a member of the 2007 4A Texas State Football Championship Team, (three-year Letterman). He also participated in track & field, winning numerous gold medals in the 100 yard dash. Jeremy held two retreats on the campus of Bay Ridge College for his teammates, sharing with them why "choices matter". Jeremy has also won the University of Iowa's Certificate of Merit during the University's Summer Journalism Camp.

The oldest of nine siblings, Jeremy often helps with homework and mentoring. He is a member of Triumph Champion Center in Richmond, TX, where he is the vice president of Generation Triumph (GT) Youth Group. As a participant in the Alpha Phi Alpha, Alpha Merit 2010 Beautillion, he won the Academic Scholar award for his essay on the *The Challenges Facing African American Males Today*.

Jeremy has been accepted into the University of Texas Austin, where he plans to earn a Bachelor of Science degree in psychology.

Jeremy D. Simmons

Senior
Lamar Consolidated High

Jordin N. Taylor

Sophomore
Bellaire High School

Jordin Taylor is a sophomore at Bellaire High School. Upon graduation, Jordin plans on attending college at either University of Texas (Austin) or Franciscan University. She aspires to become a pharmacist and/or a retail buyer.

Jordin's achievements include the (2011) first place winner in the case competition for Leaders of Tomorrow, (2010) third place winner in the case competition for Leaders of Tomorrow, (2009) award for acts of kindness, (2009) award for attendance and the (2009) award for academics. Jordin was also nominated by her teacher for the 2011 United States Achievement Academy.

Jordin's school activities include Bellaire Women's lacrosse, dance and African American Association. Her volunteer work consists of M.D. Anderson Hospital, Texas Children's Hospital, City Wide Club and Star of Hope. Jordin continues to be an active member of The National Black MBA Leaders of Tomorrow and she is a faithful member of St. Thomas More Catholic Church, where she also attended school while in junior high. Her parents are Rod and Ramona Taylor.

Jibraun Wilson

Senior
Hightower High School

Jibraun Wilson is a senior at Hightower High School in Missouri City, Texas. He serves on the Youth Usher Ministry at the Fort Bend Church and is a member of the High School College Ministry.

He is a member of the Humble Intercontinental Chapter of Top Teens of America, Inc. and currently serves as Sergeant at Arms. Jibraun was named Mr. Top Teen 2010-2011, and his experience with Top Teens has taught him the importance of leadership and serving the community.

Jibraun is an active member of the Leaders of Tomorrow (LOT) Program sponsored by the Houston Chapter of the Black MBA Association. Participation in the annual LOT Case competition has taught him leadership, presentation and analytical skills. He has attended the National Black MBA Conference in Washington, DC and New Orleans, Louisiana.

Jibraun plans to attend Sam Houston State University to receive a degree in business/accounting. His goal is to become a certified public accountant and entrepreneur. He is the son of Alphonso and Marcia Wilson.

We Celebrate and Support Who's Who In Black Houston

WALTER THOMAS
SALES MANAGER

STACY McINTOSH
SALES CONSULTANT

RON JENKINS
SERVICE CONSULTANT

OMAR PAYTON
SALES CONSULTANT

RODNEY WILLIAMS
SALES CONSULTANT

JAMES WIMBLEY
CUSTOMER RELATIONS MANAGER

Conveniently Located at 2520 Main Street (Main @ McGowen) • Houston, TX 77002
713.874.0900 • www.stewartcadillac.net

BIOGRAPHICAL INDEX

BIOGRAPHICAL INDEX